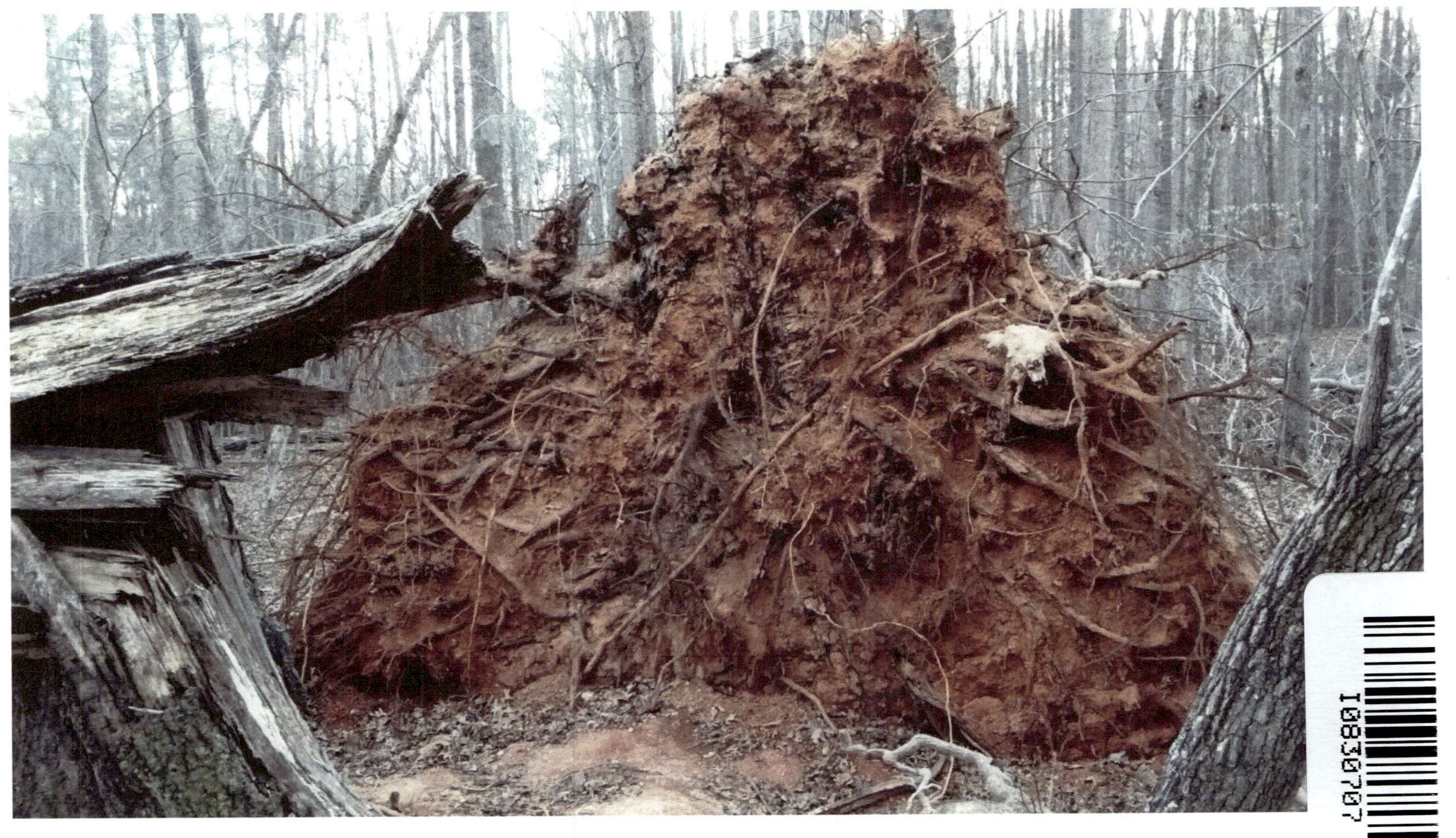

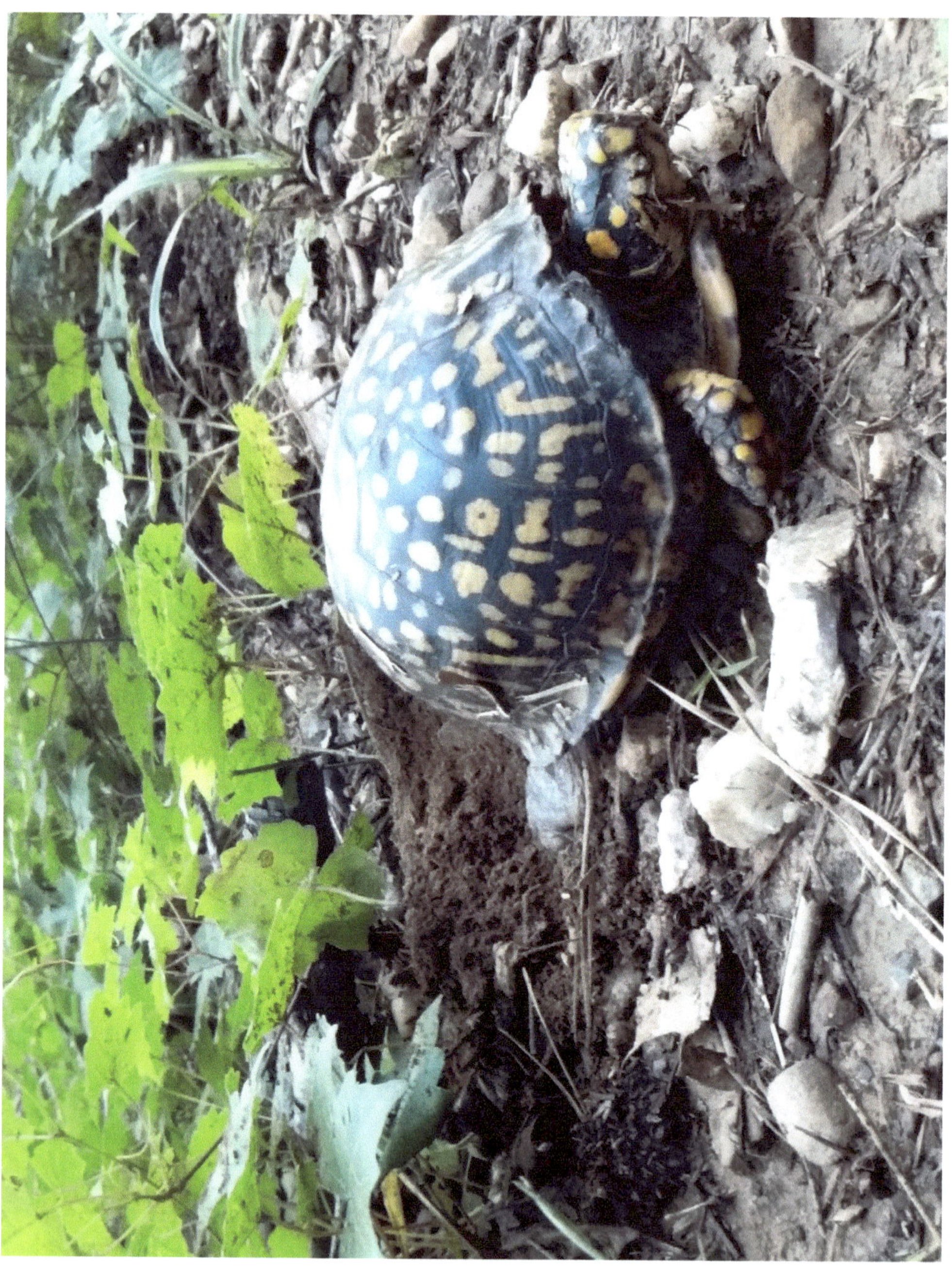

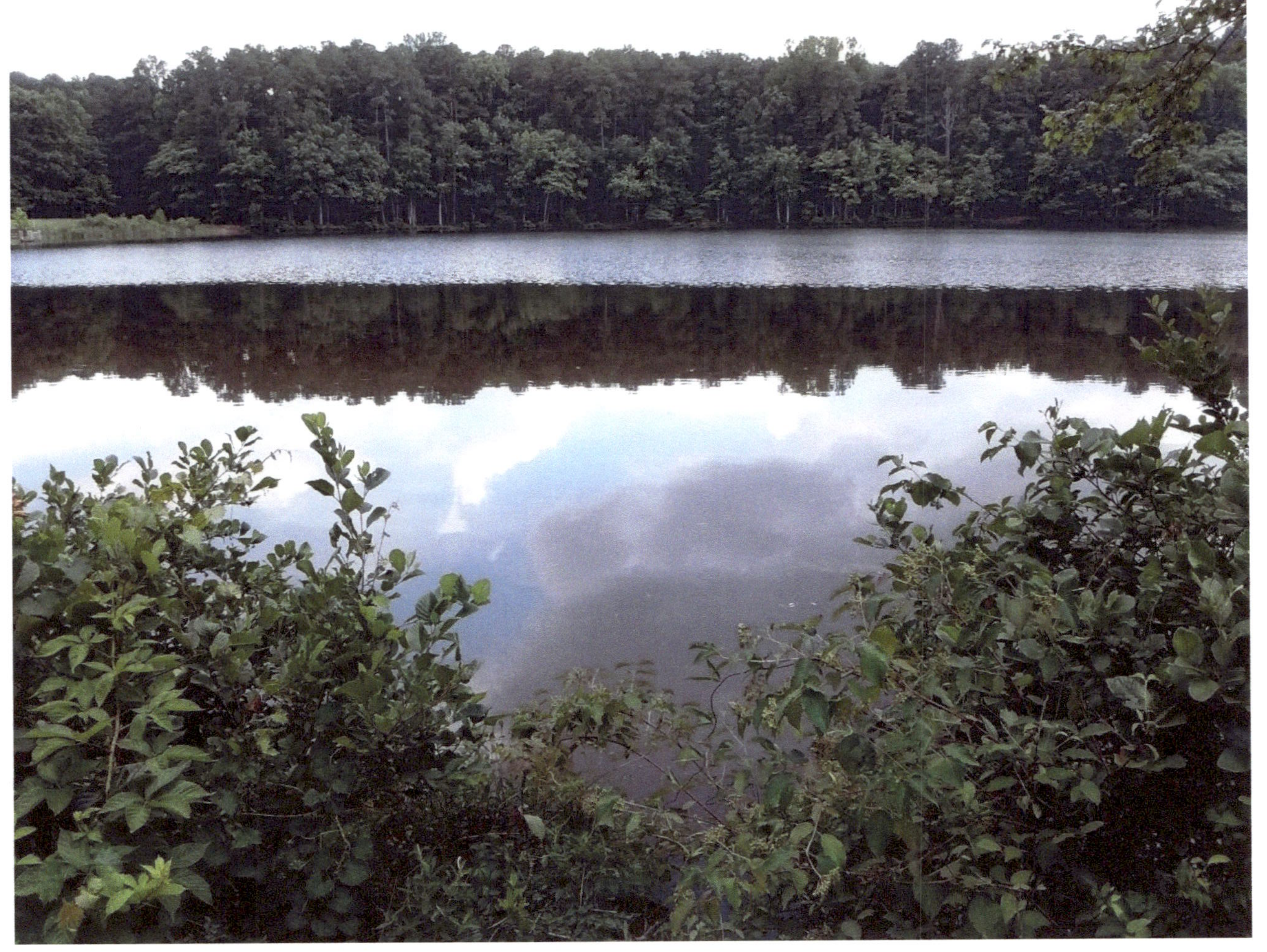

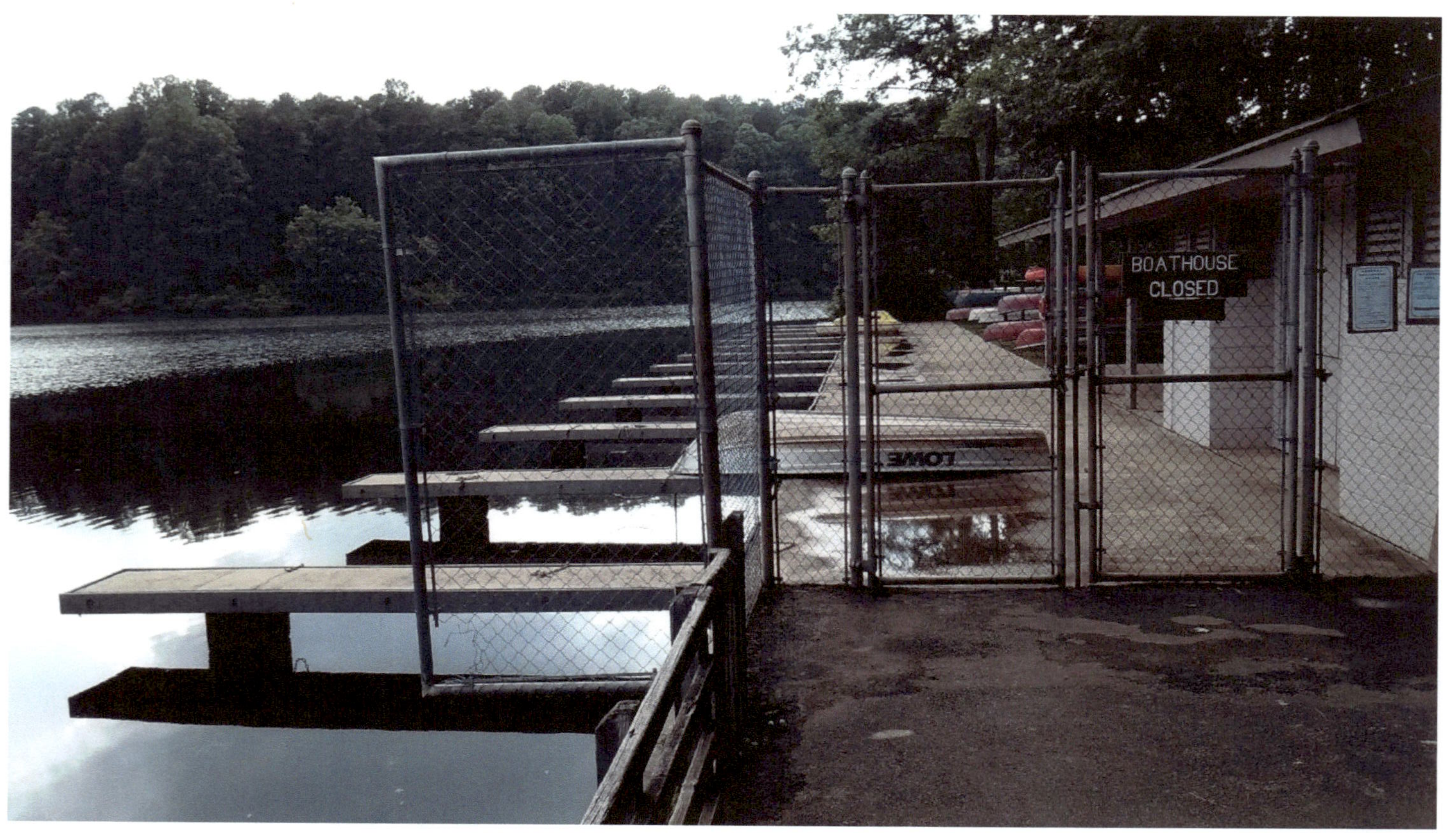

BOATHOUSE
CLOSED
LOWE

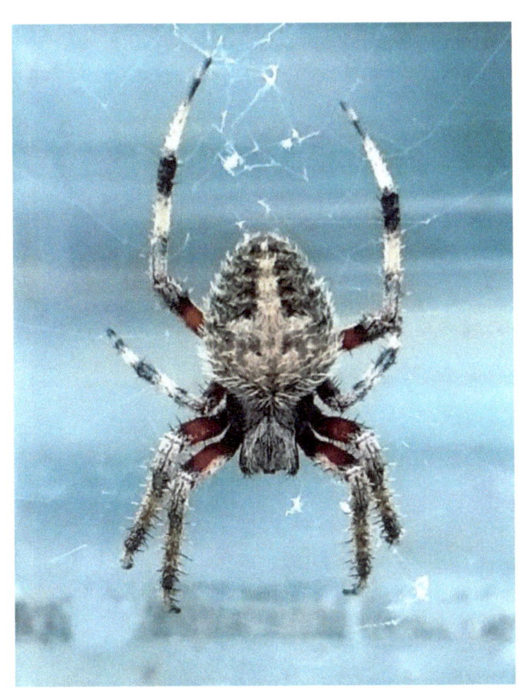

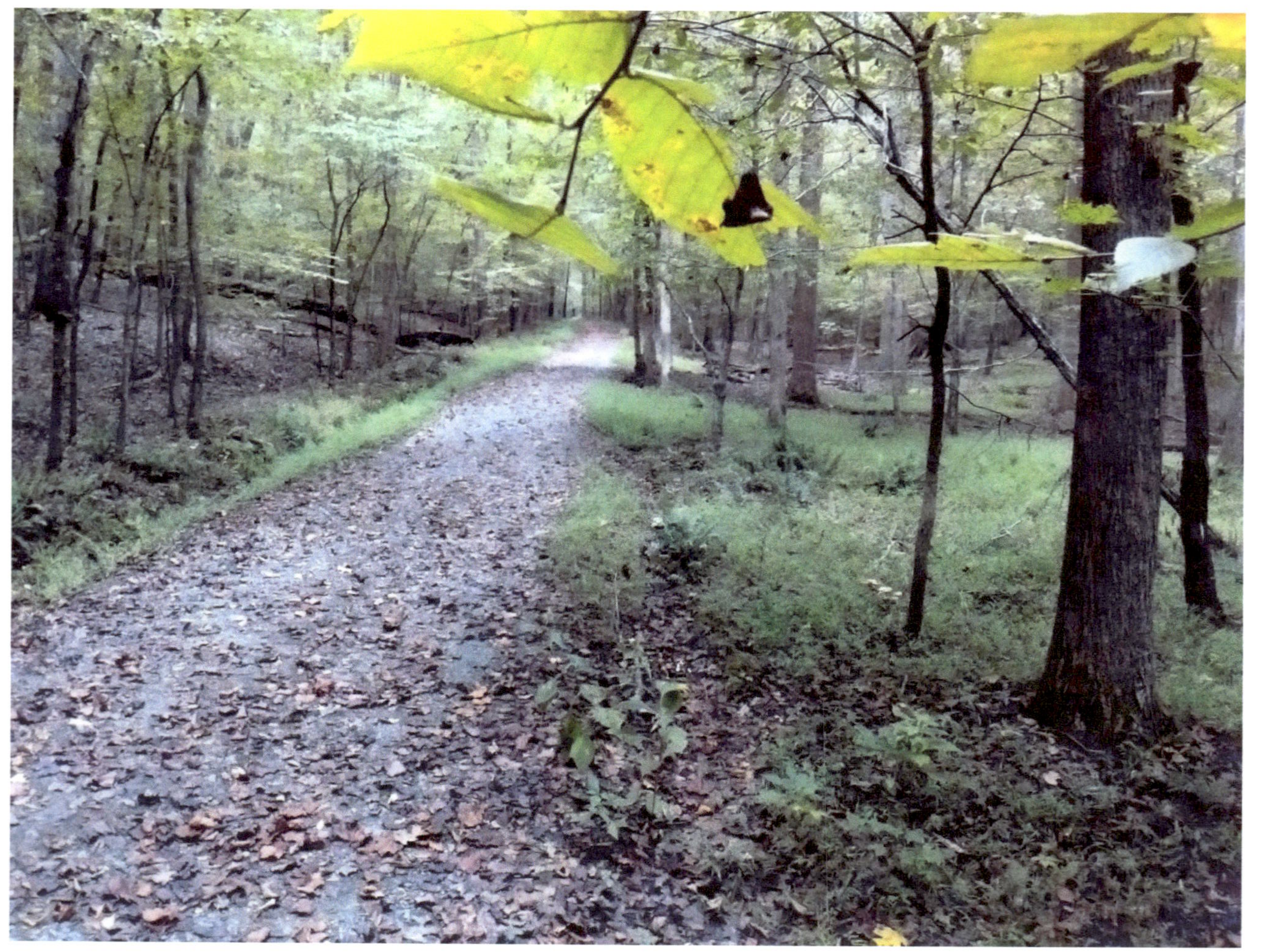

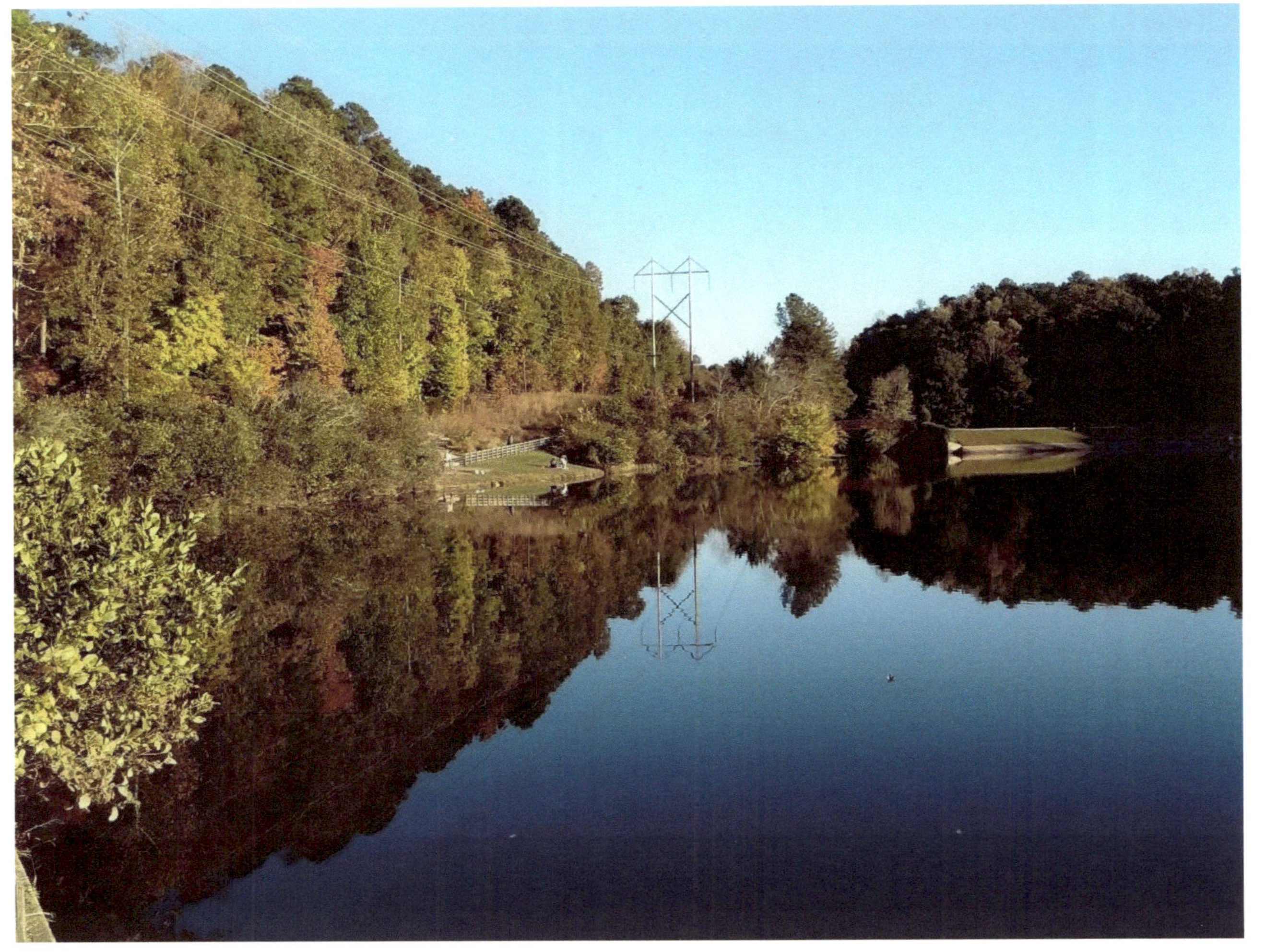

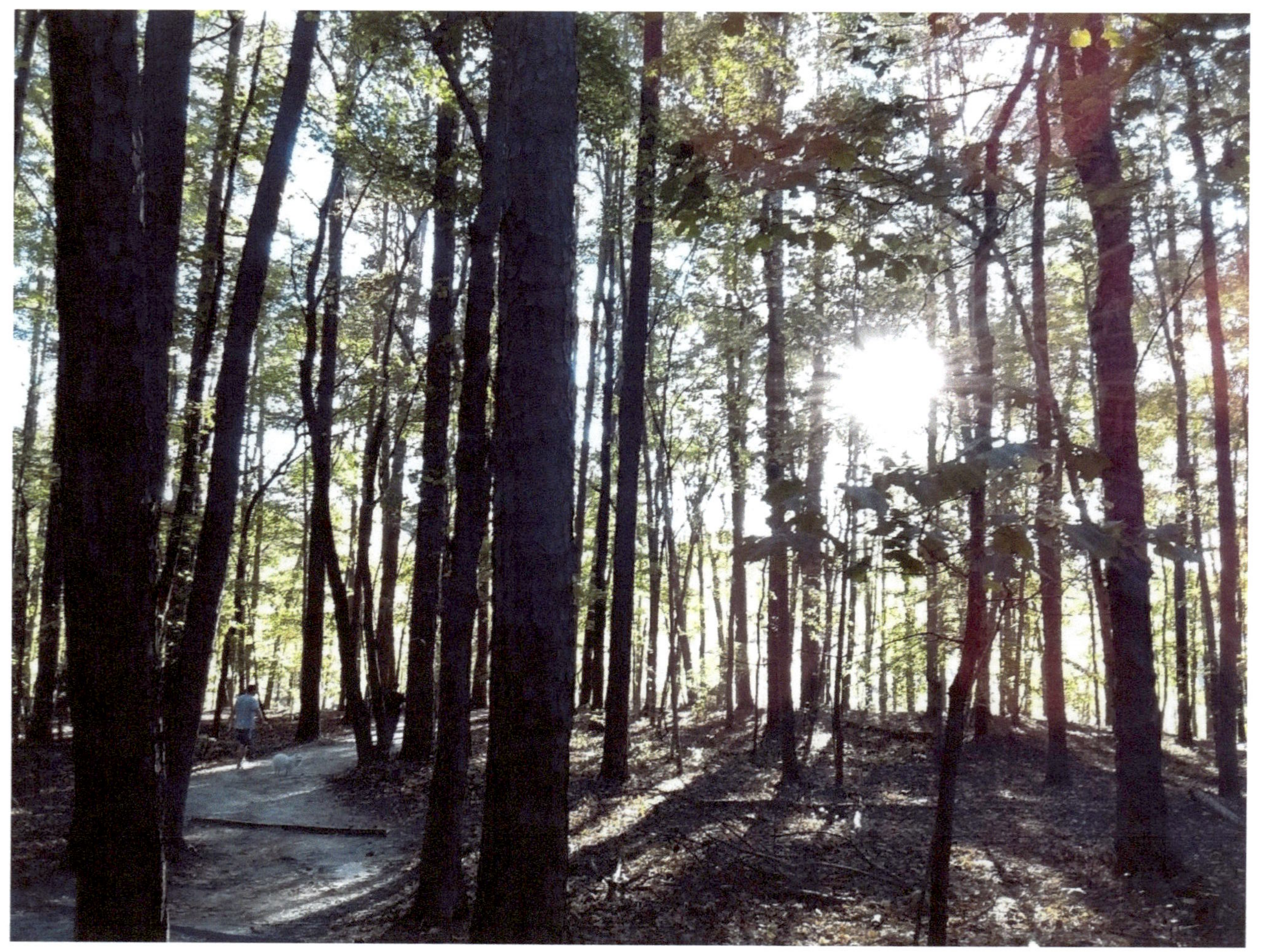

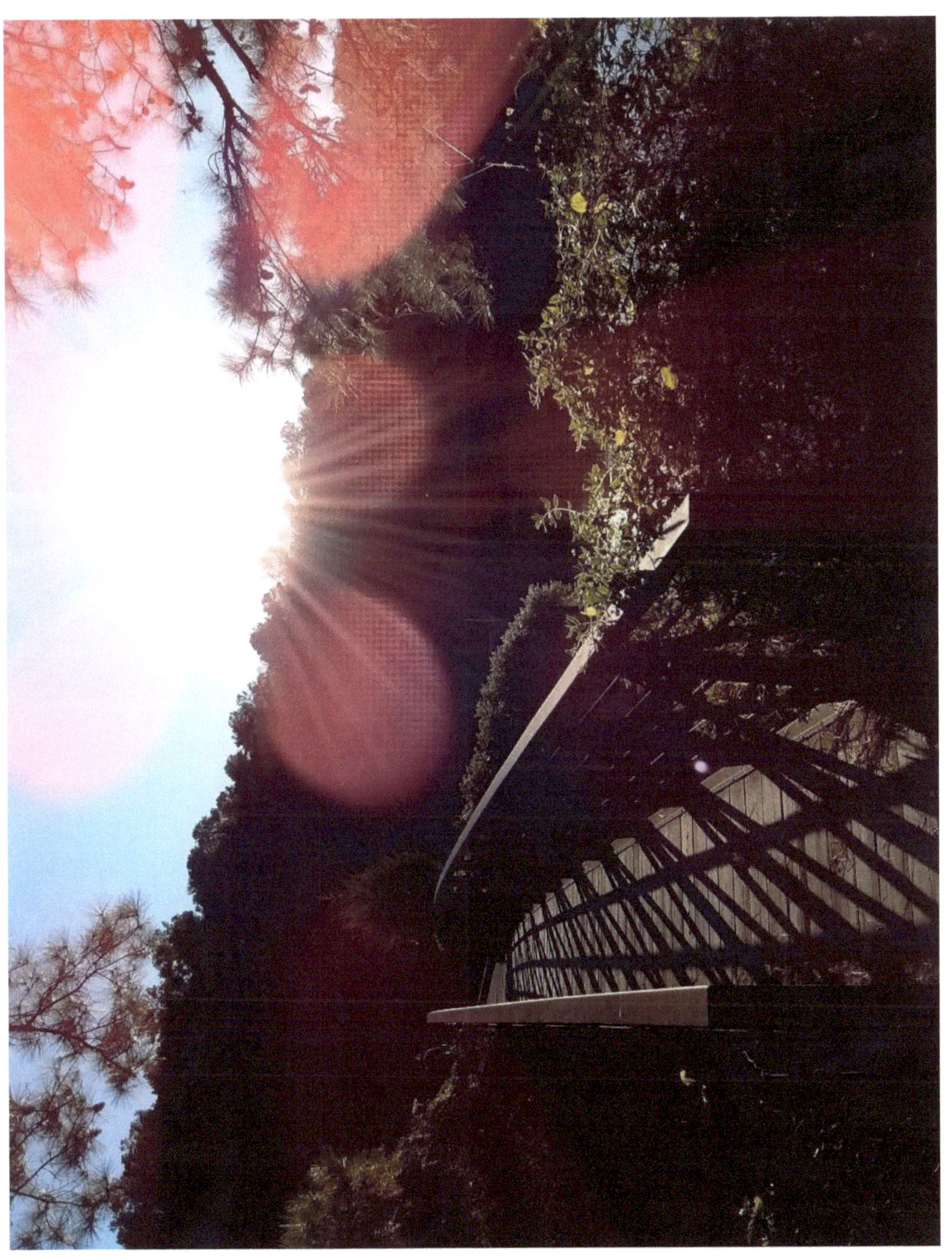

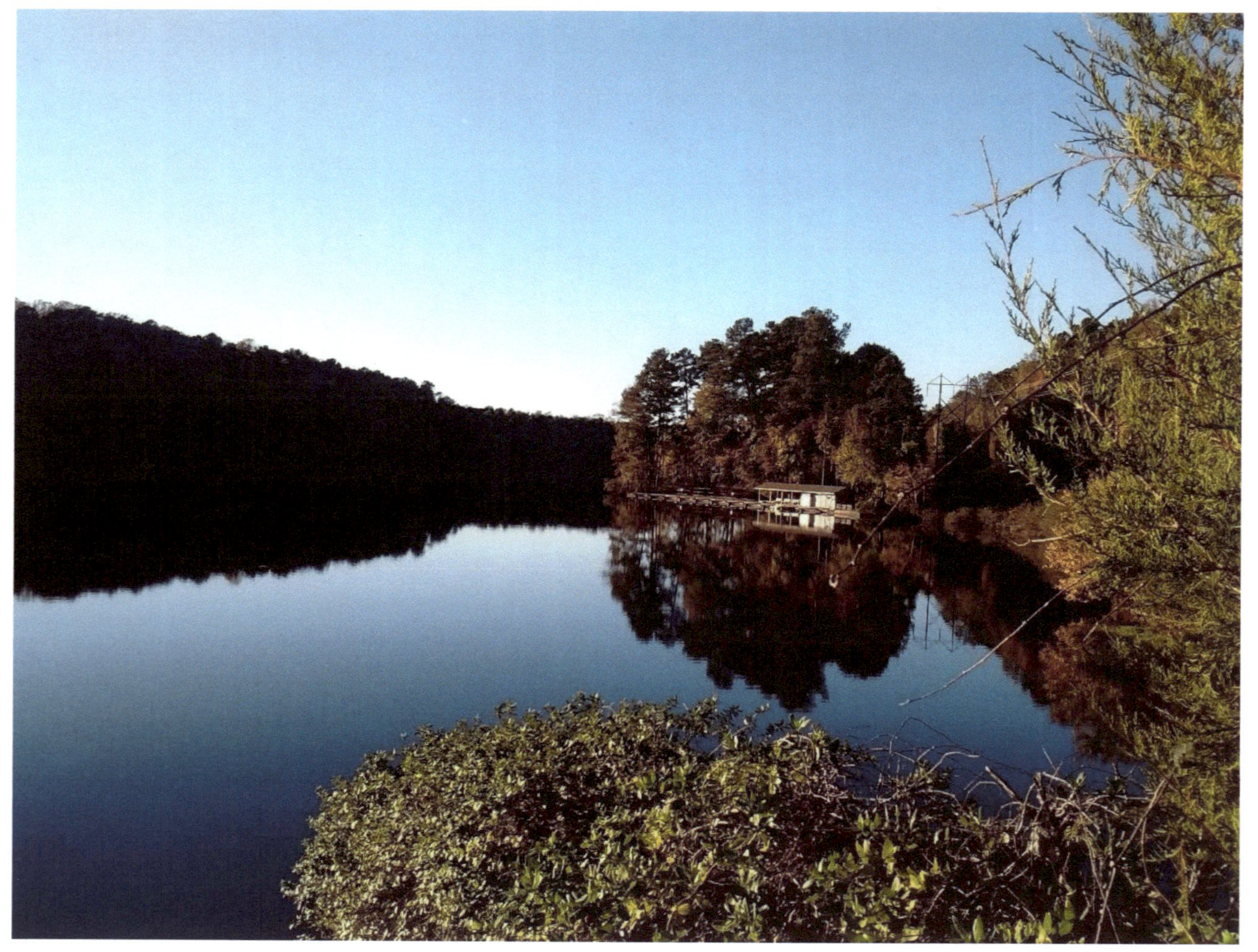

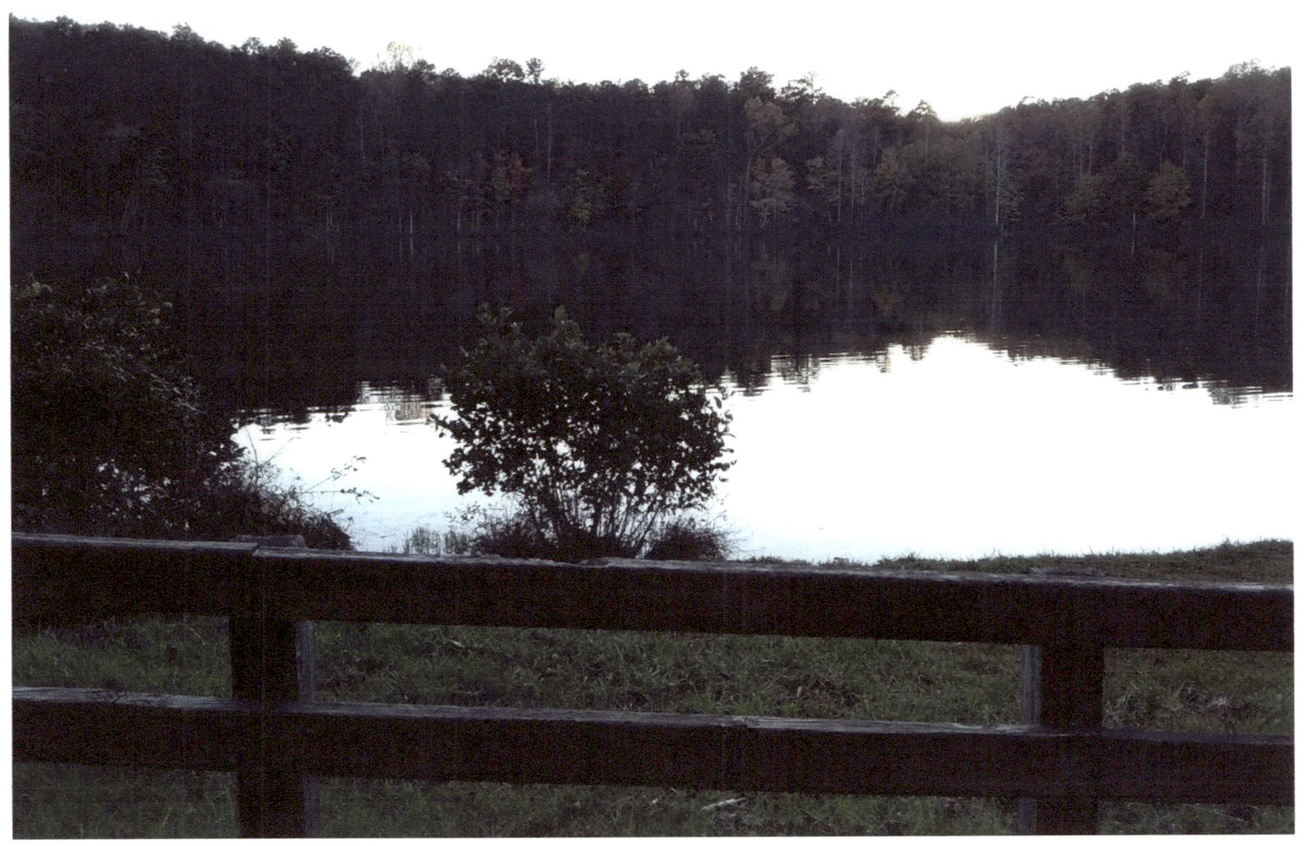

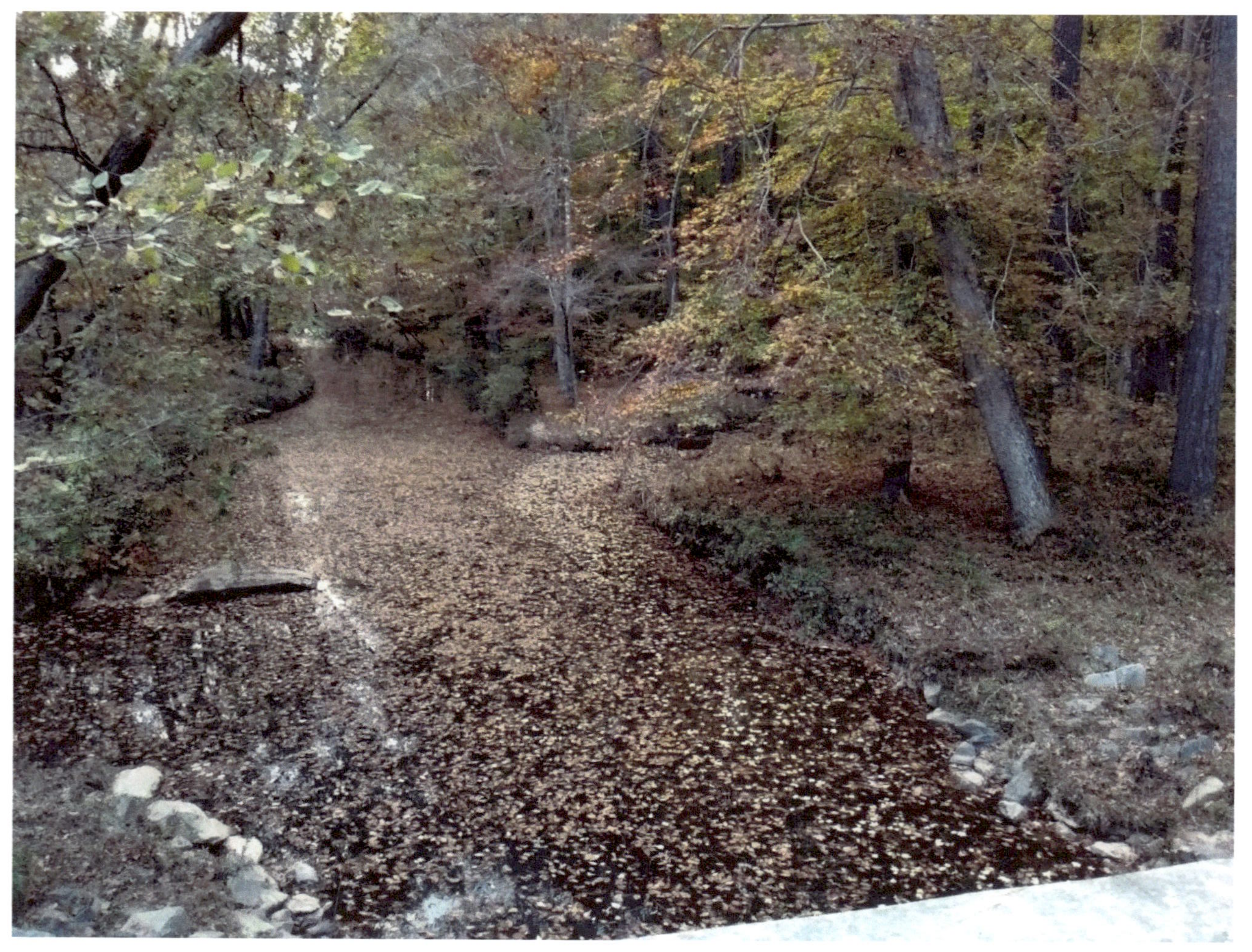

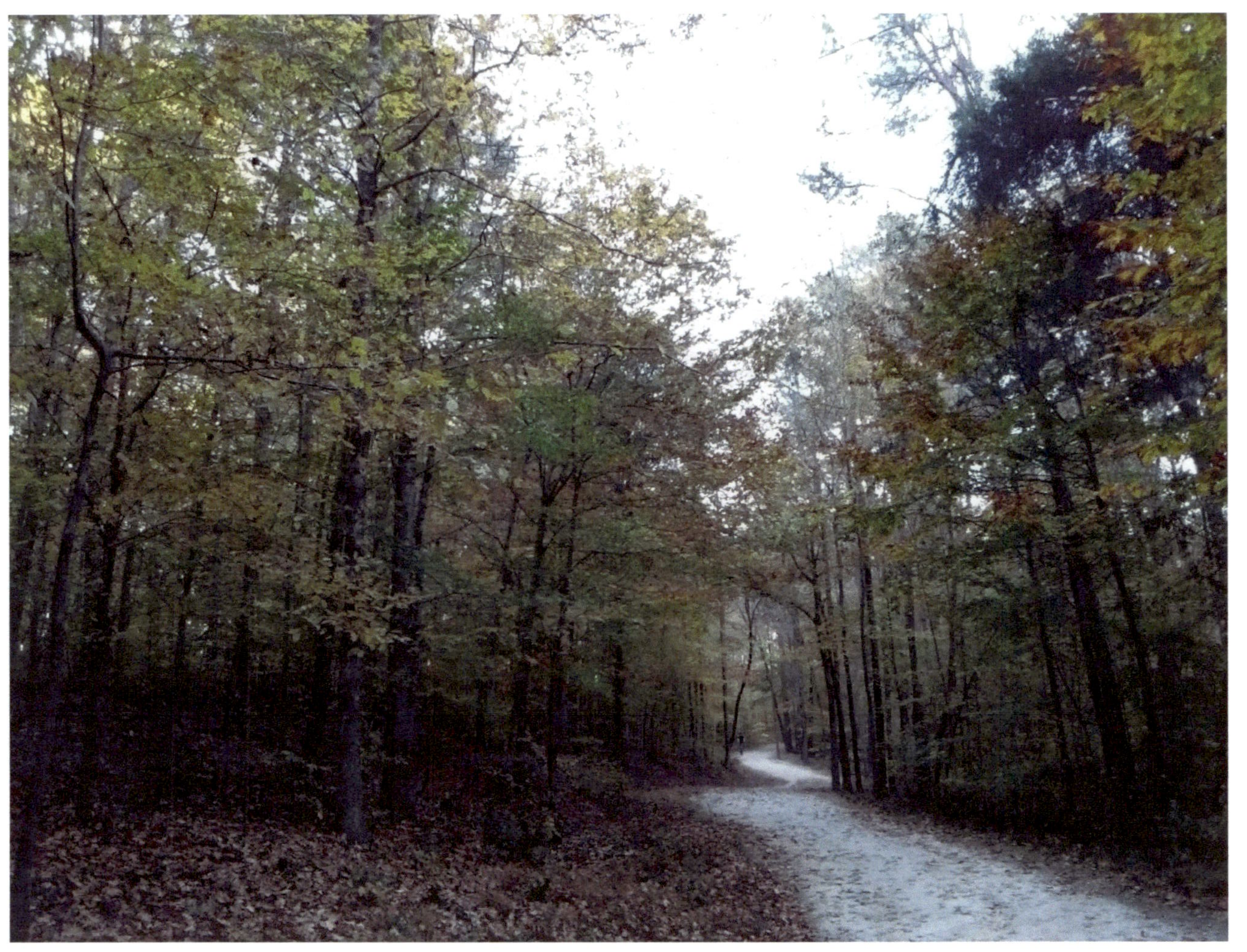

13

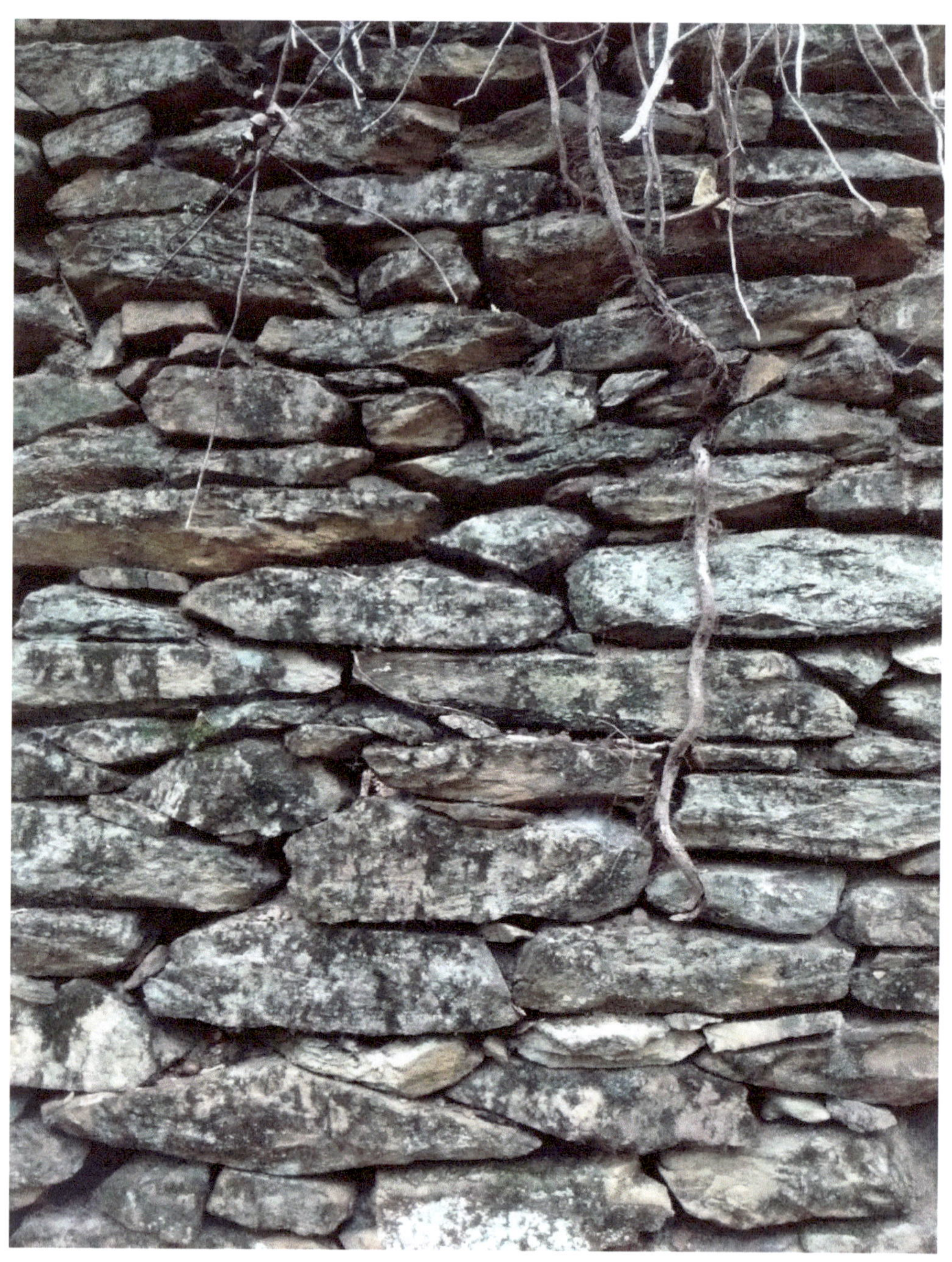

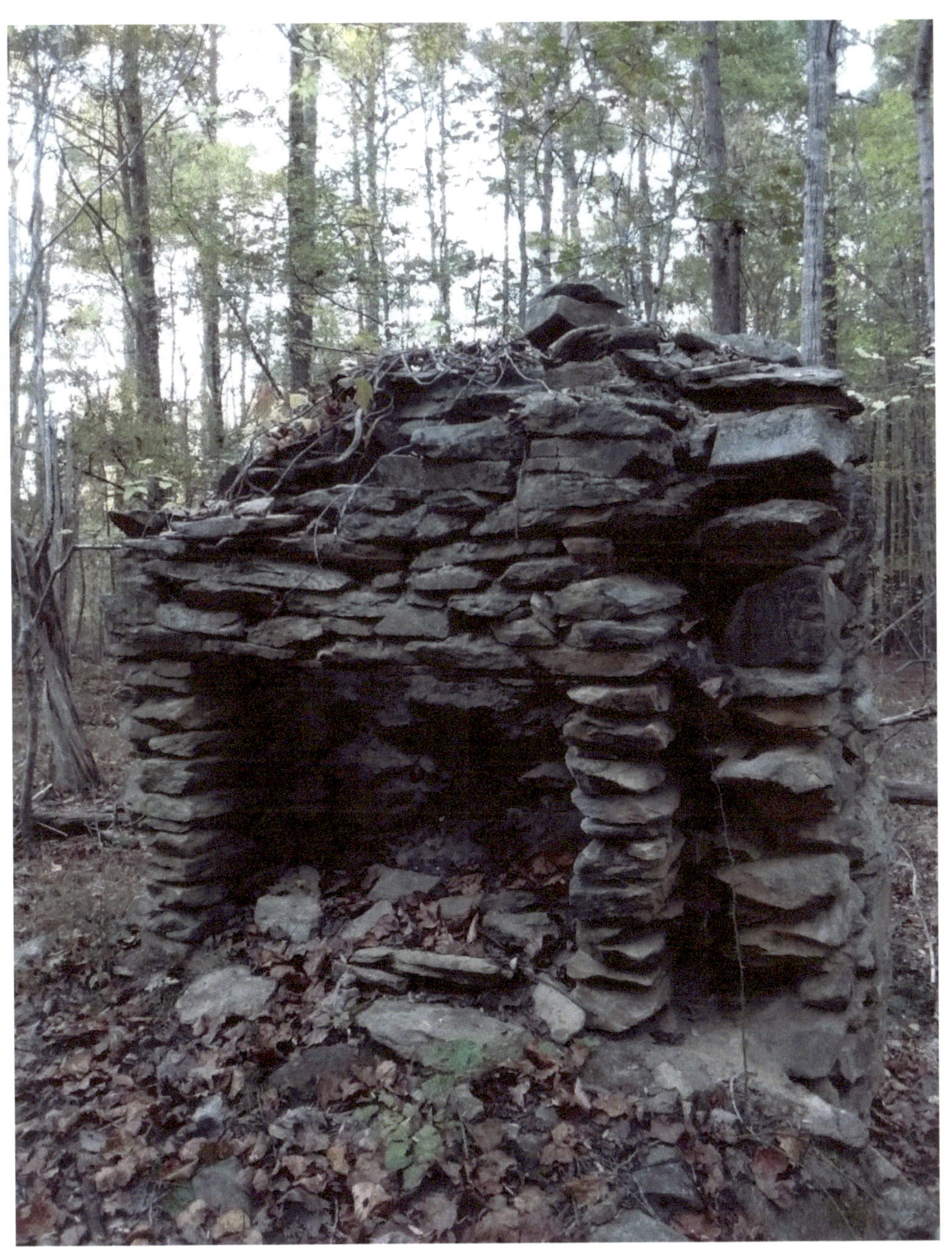

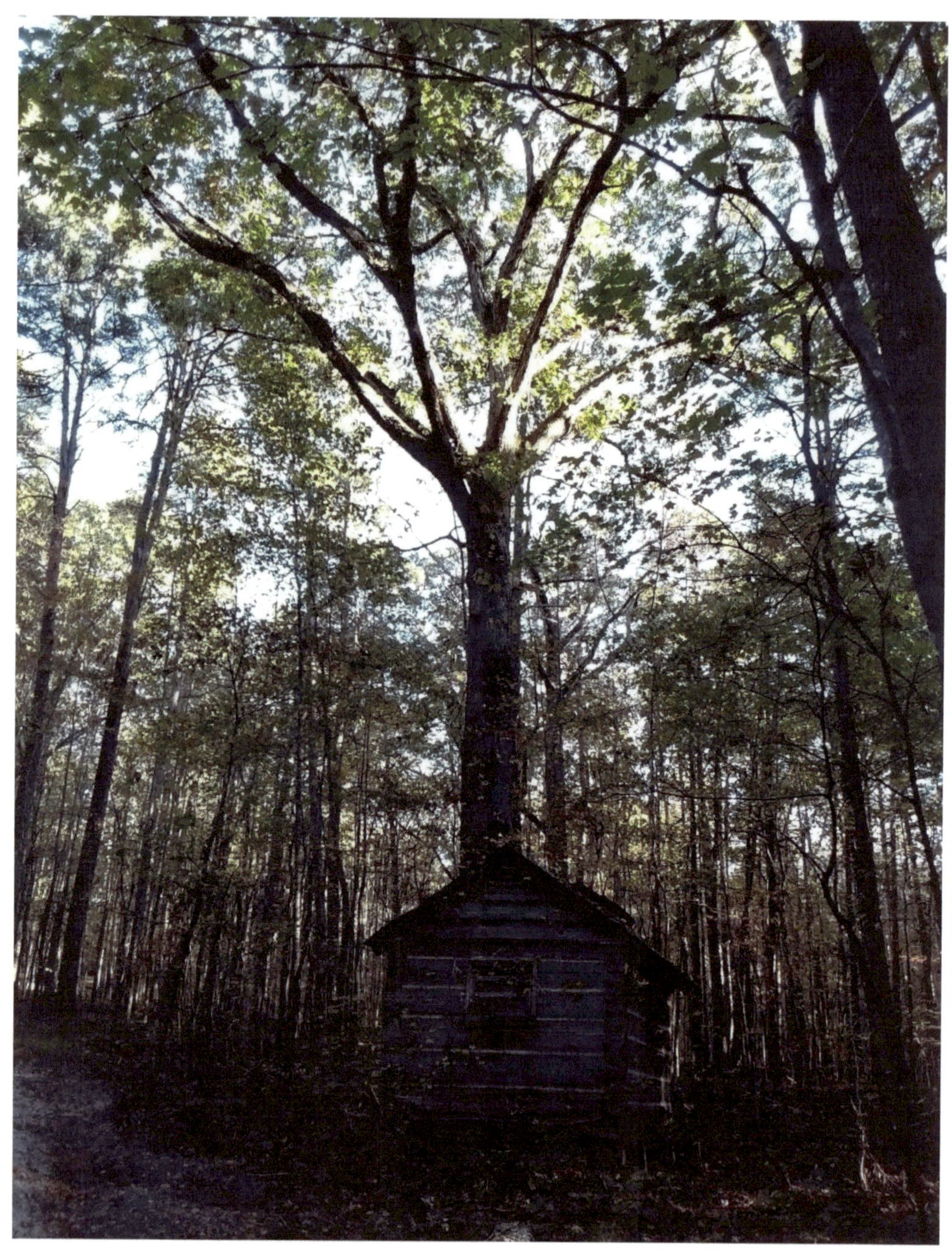

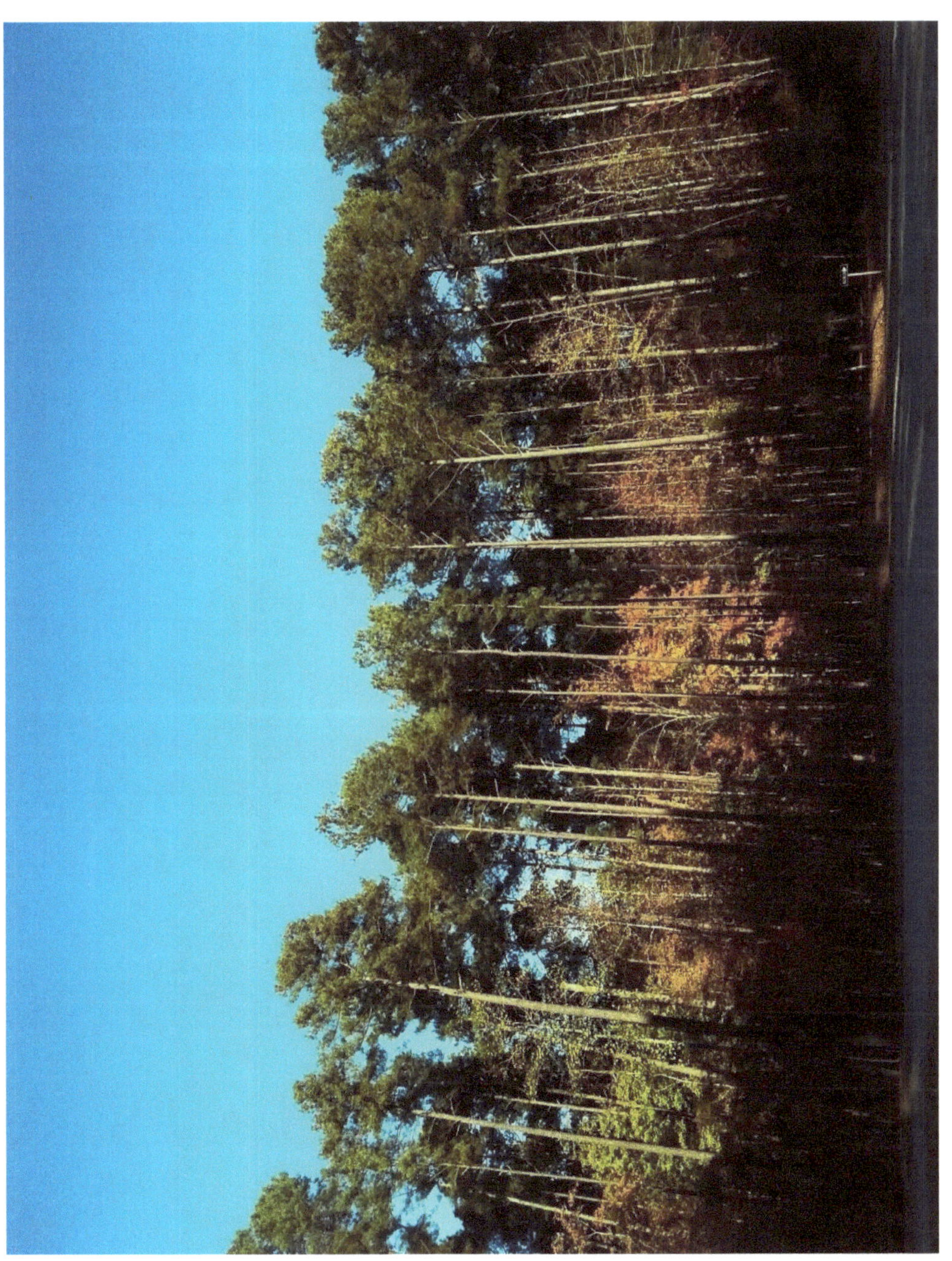

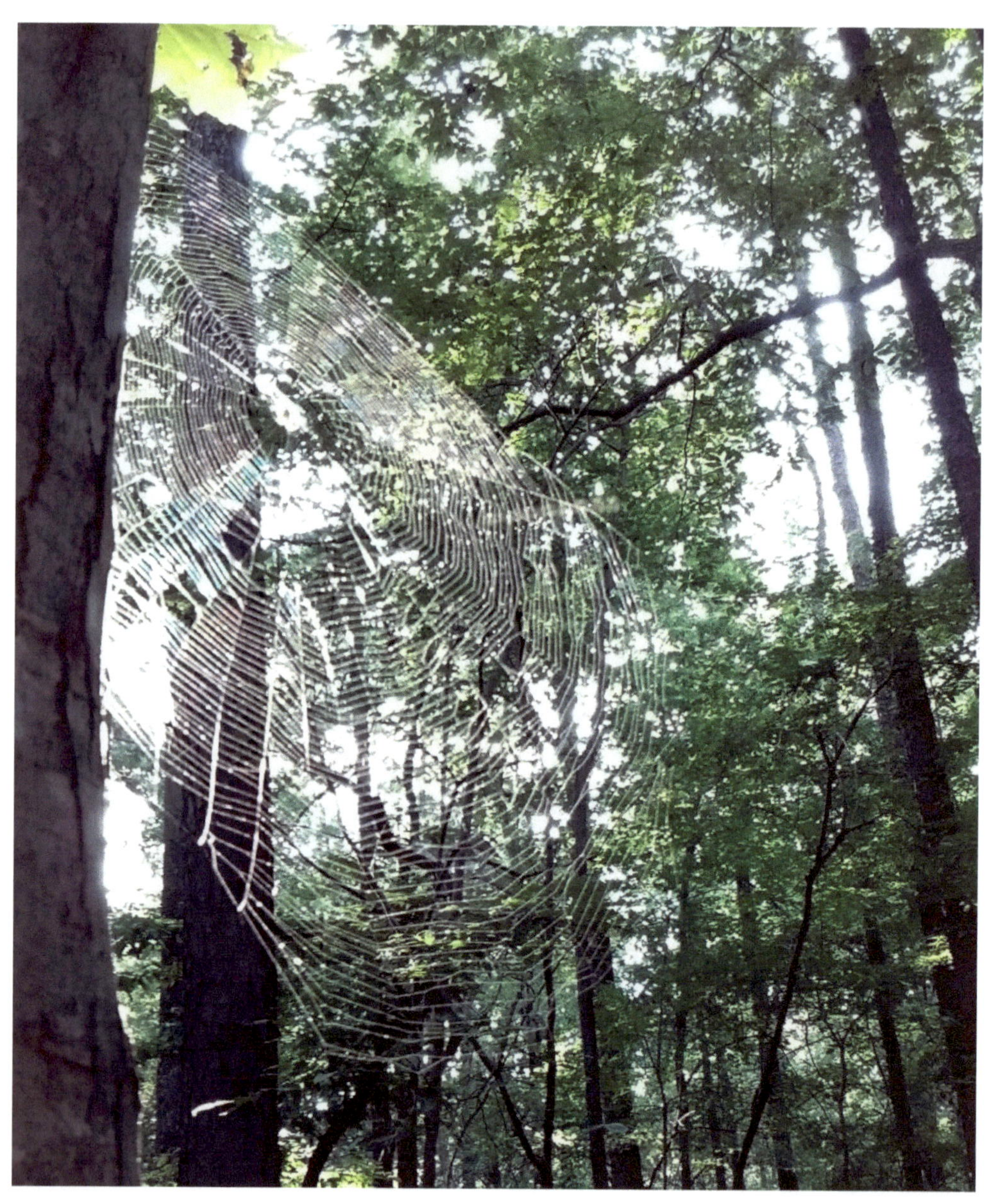

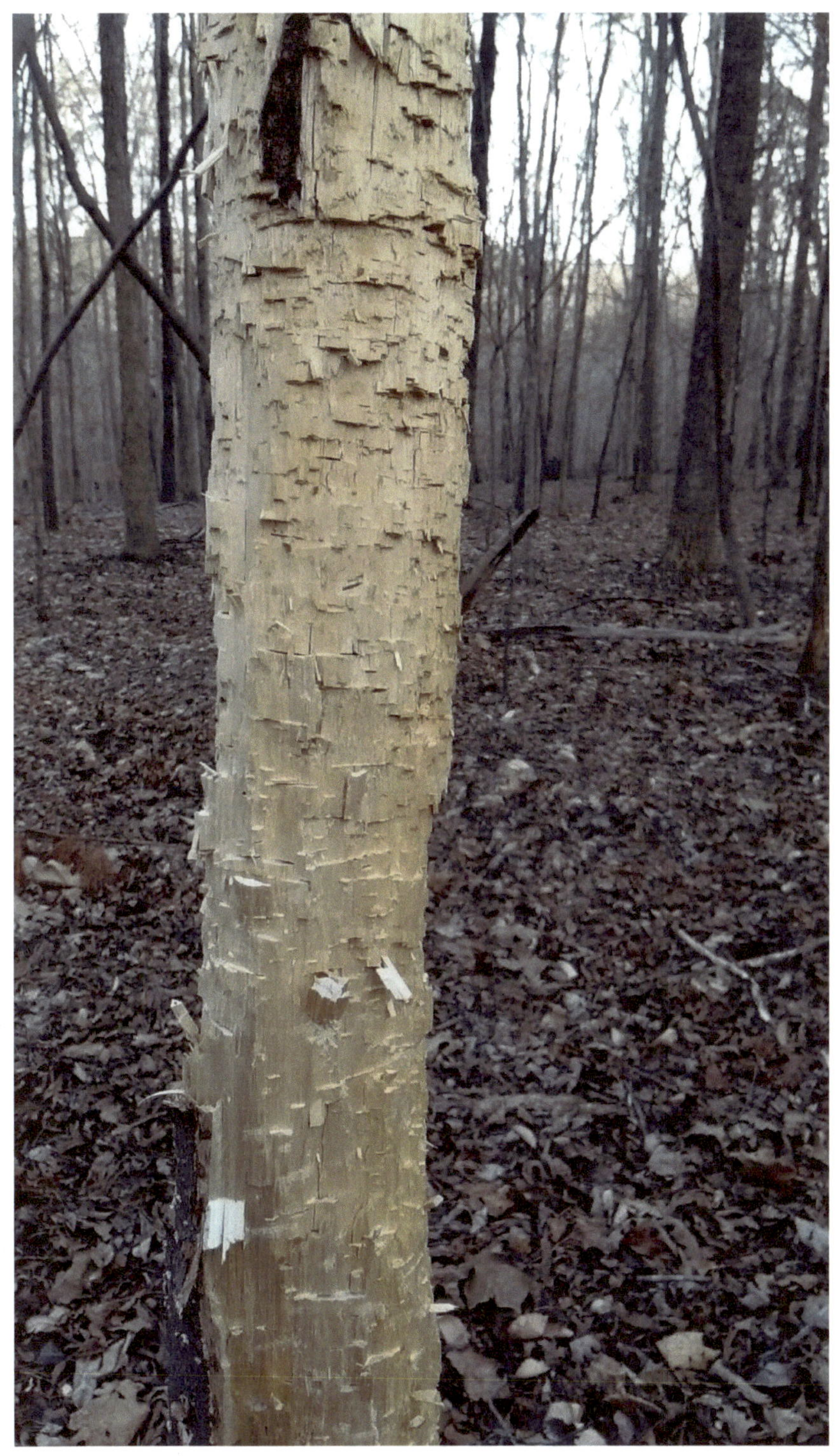

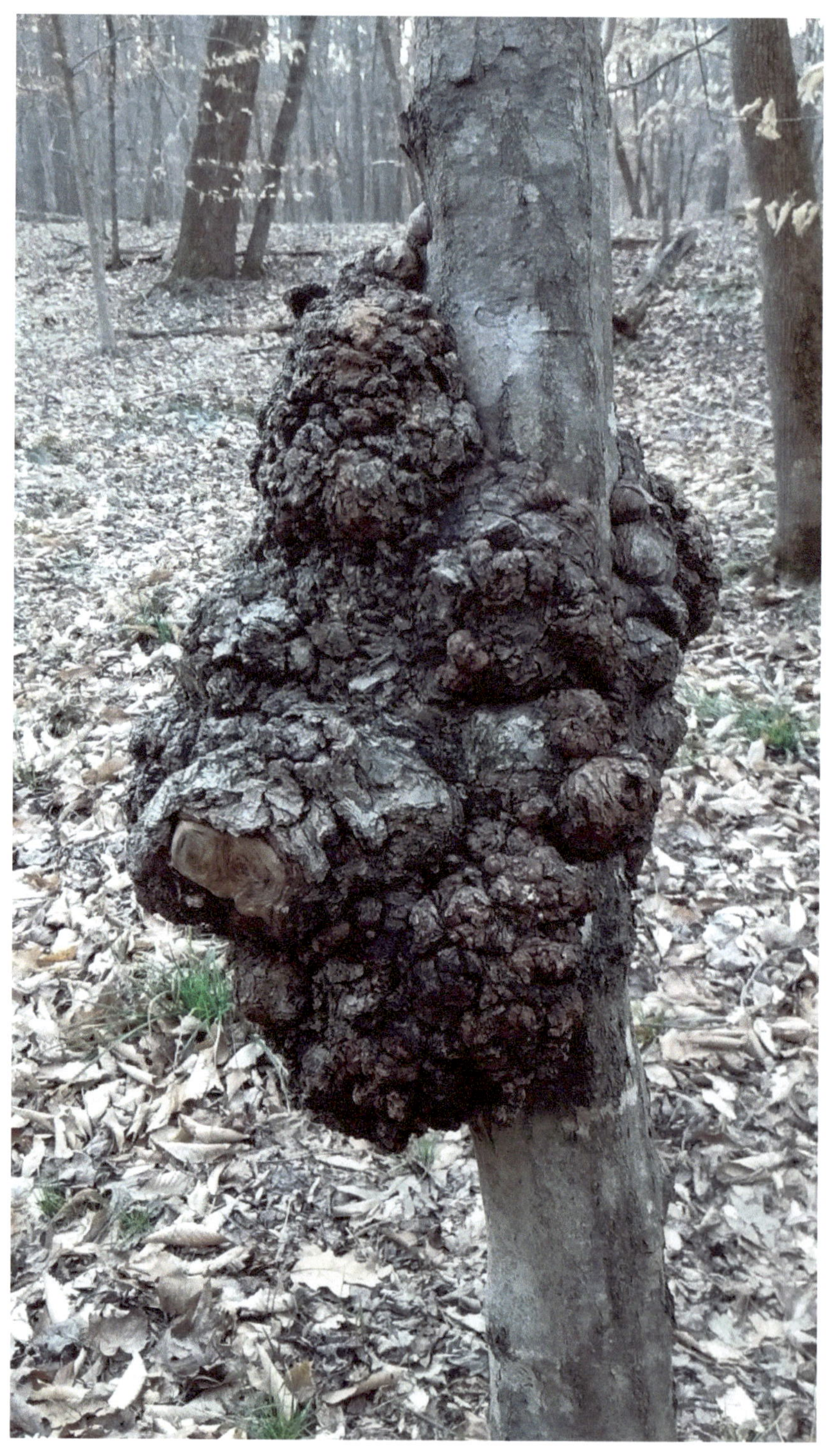

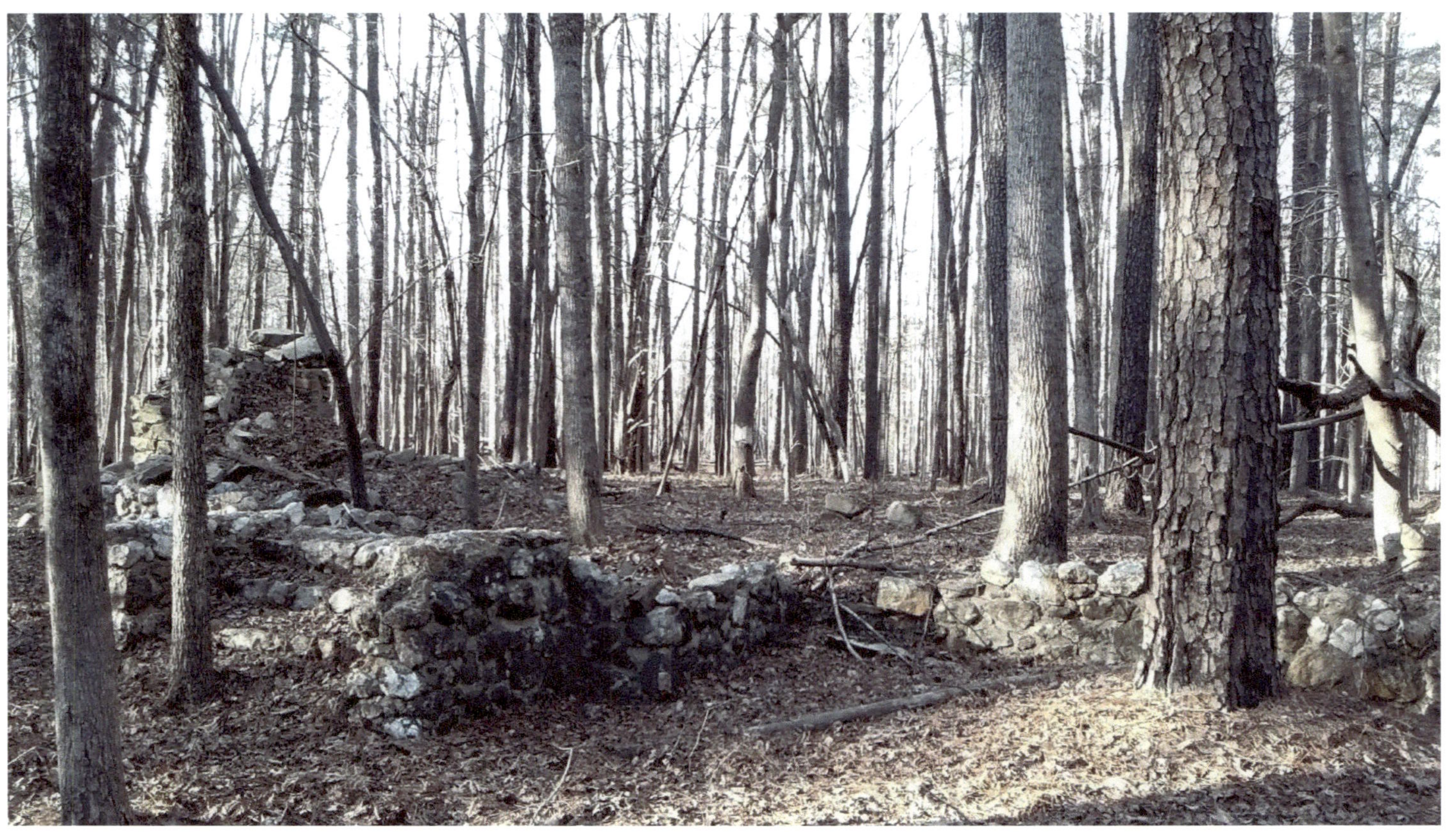

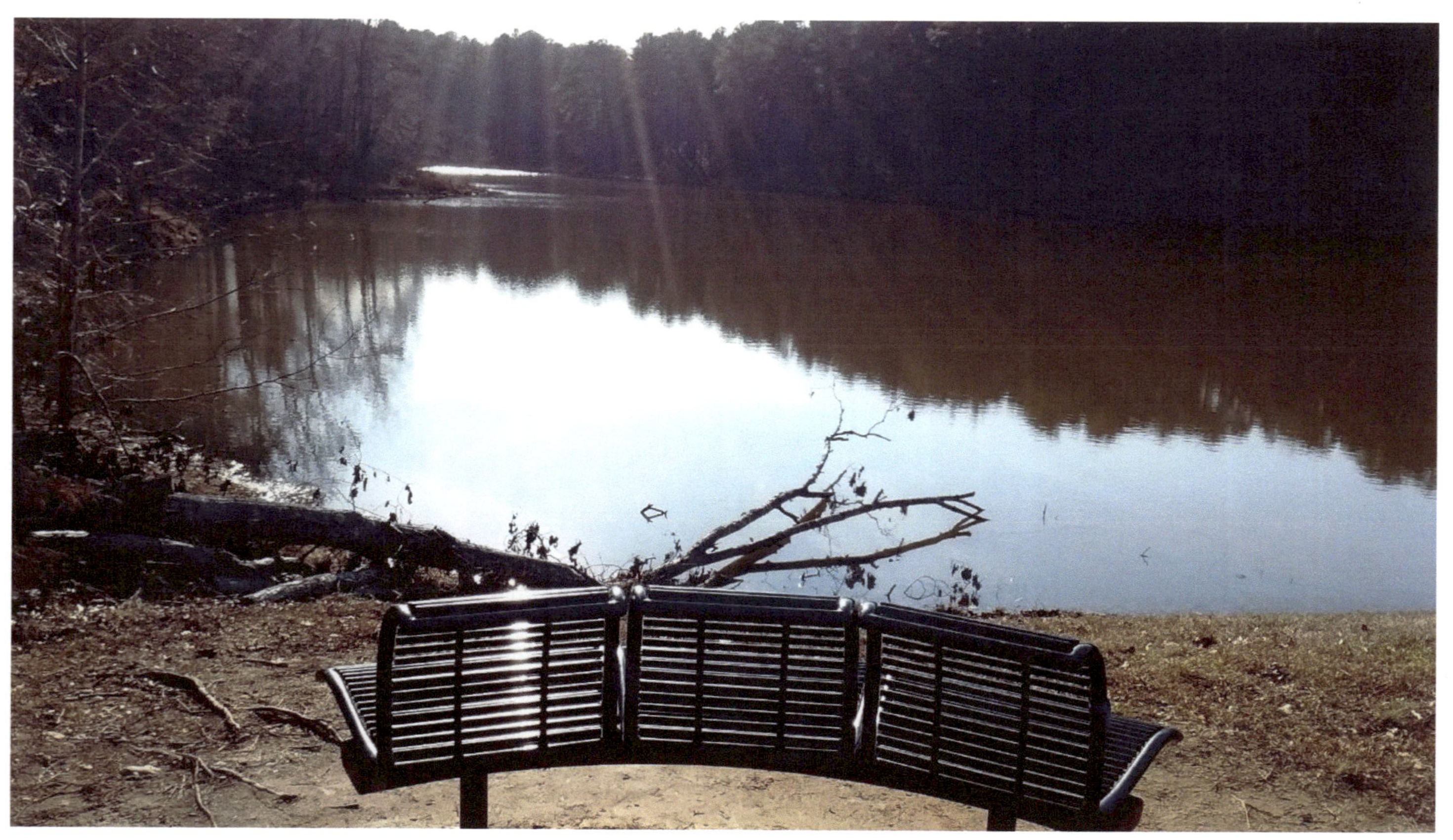

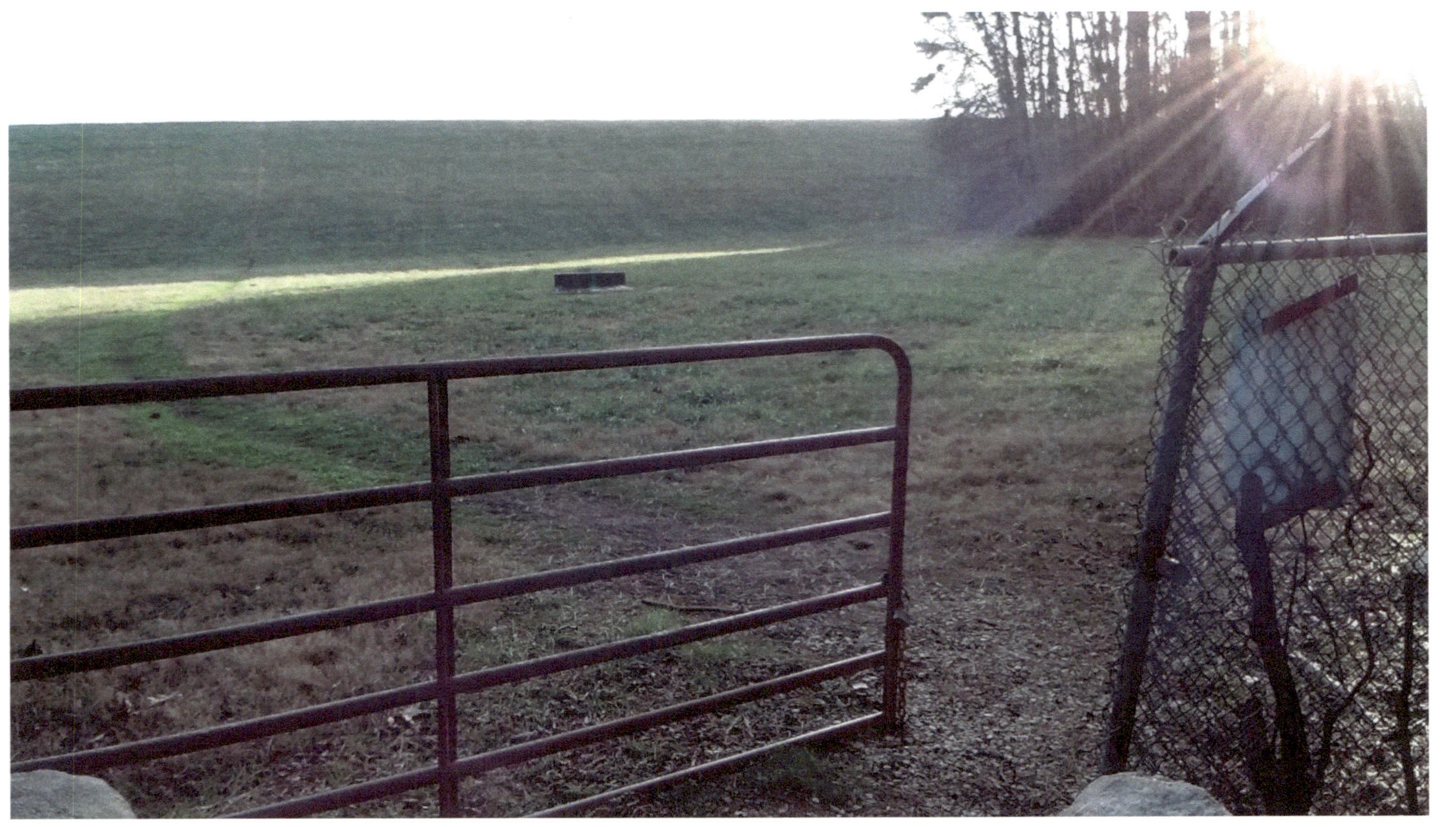

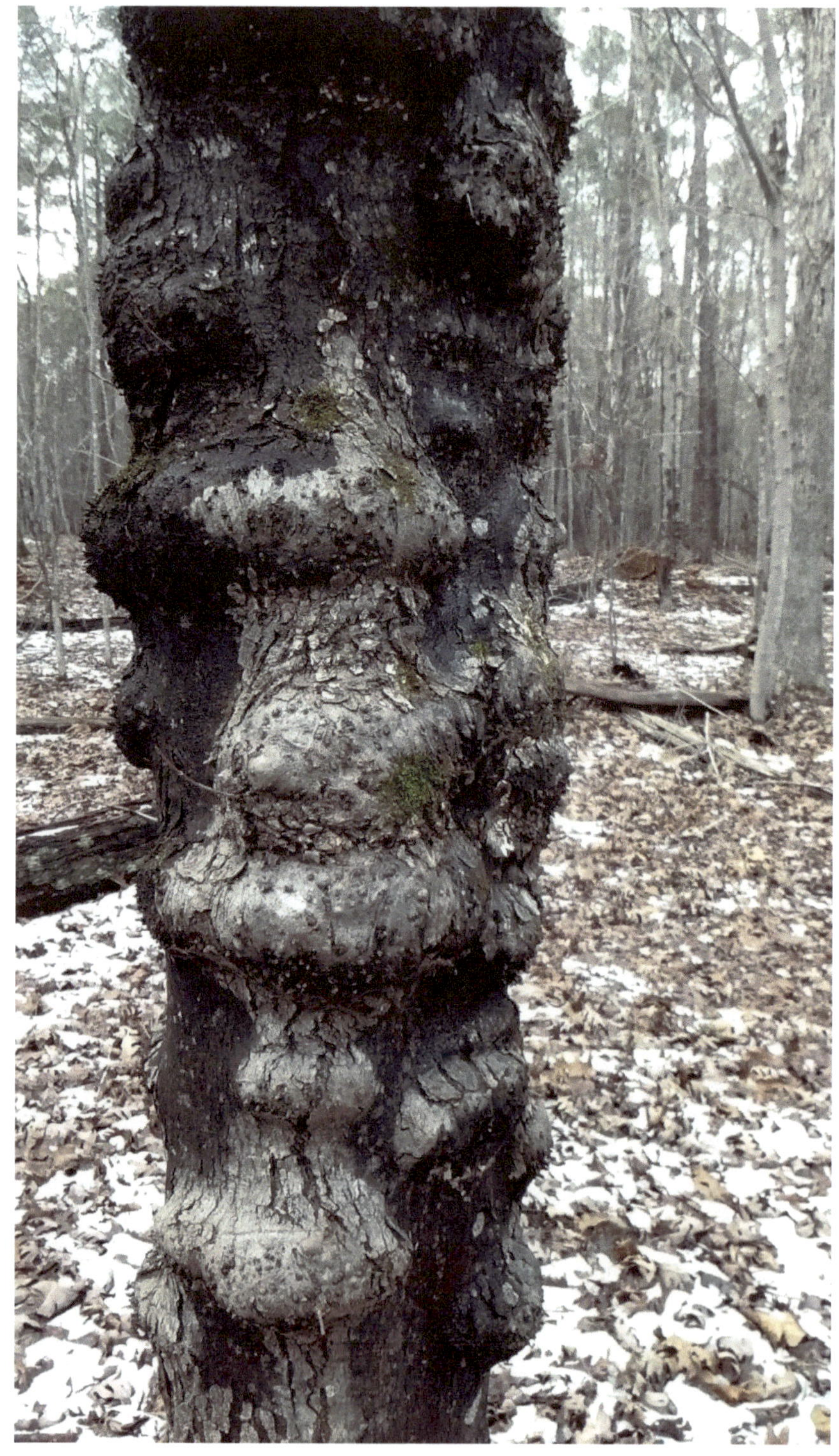

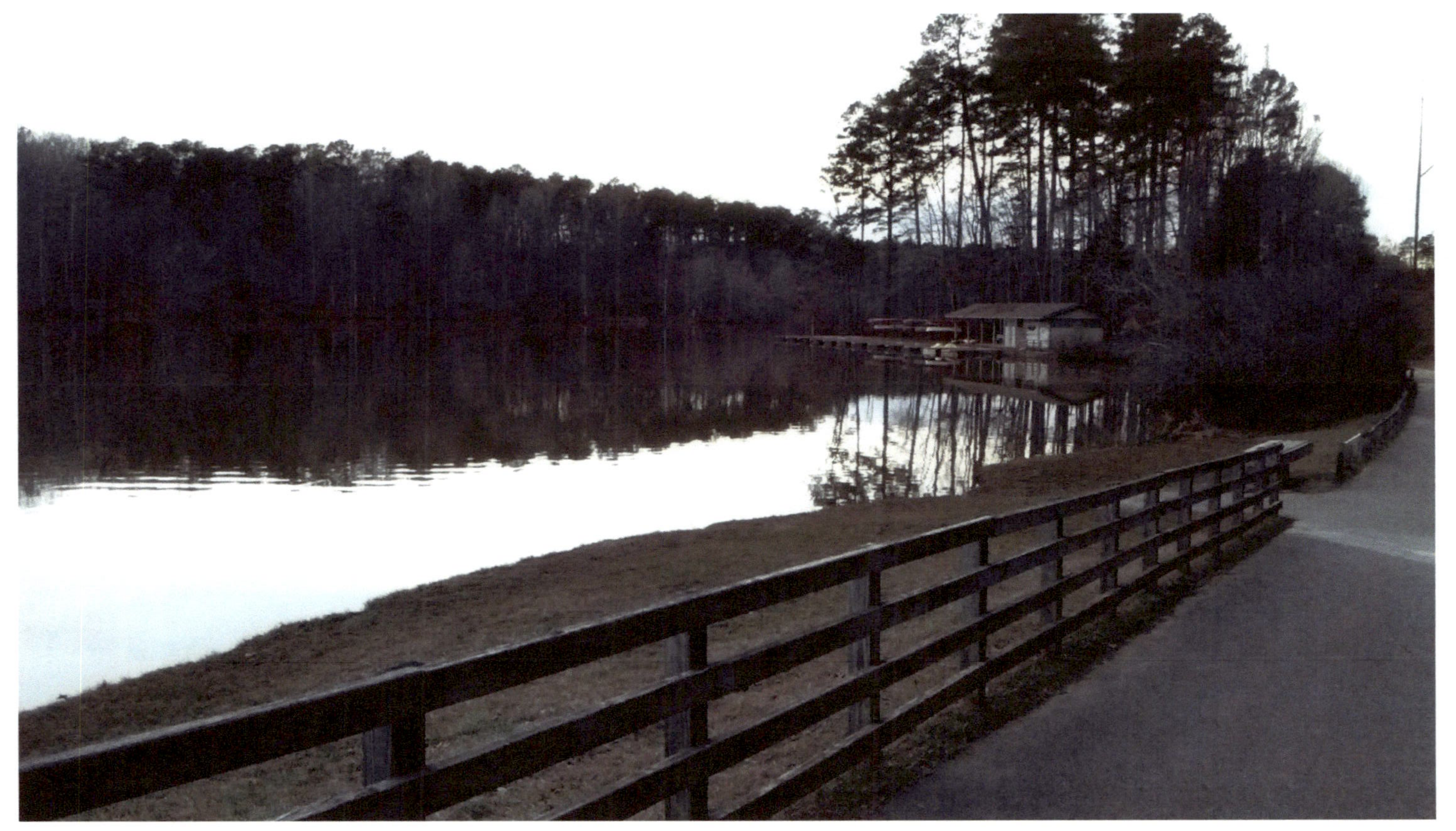

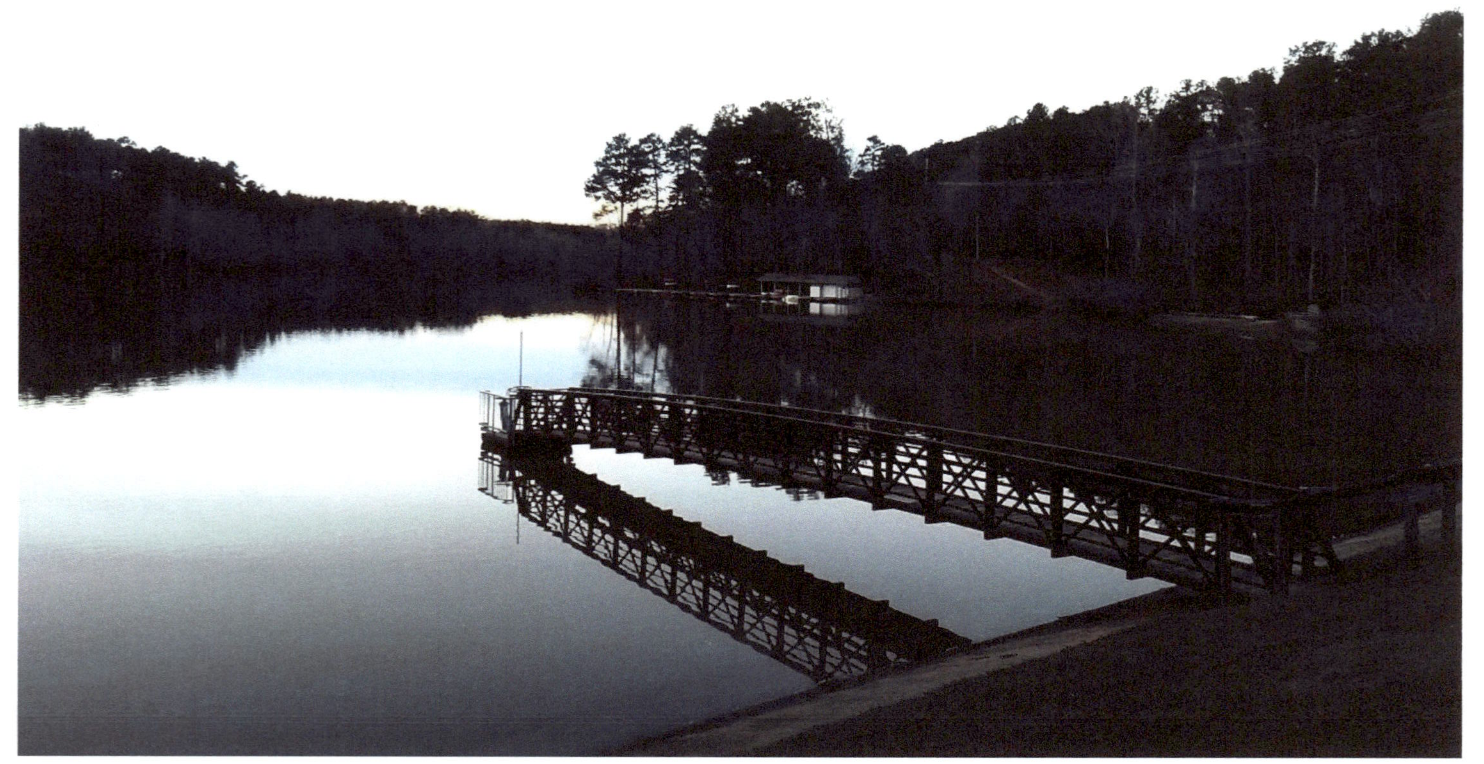

26

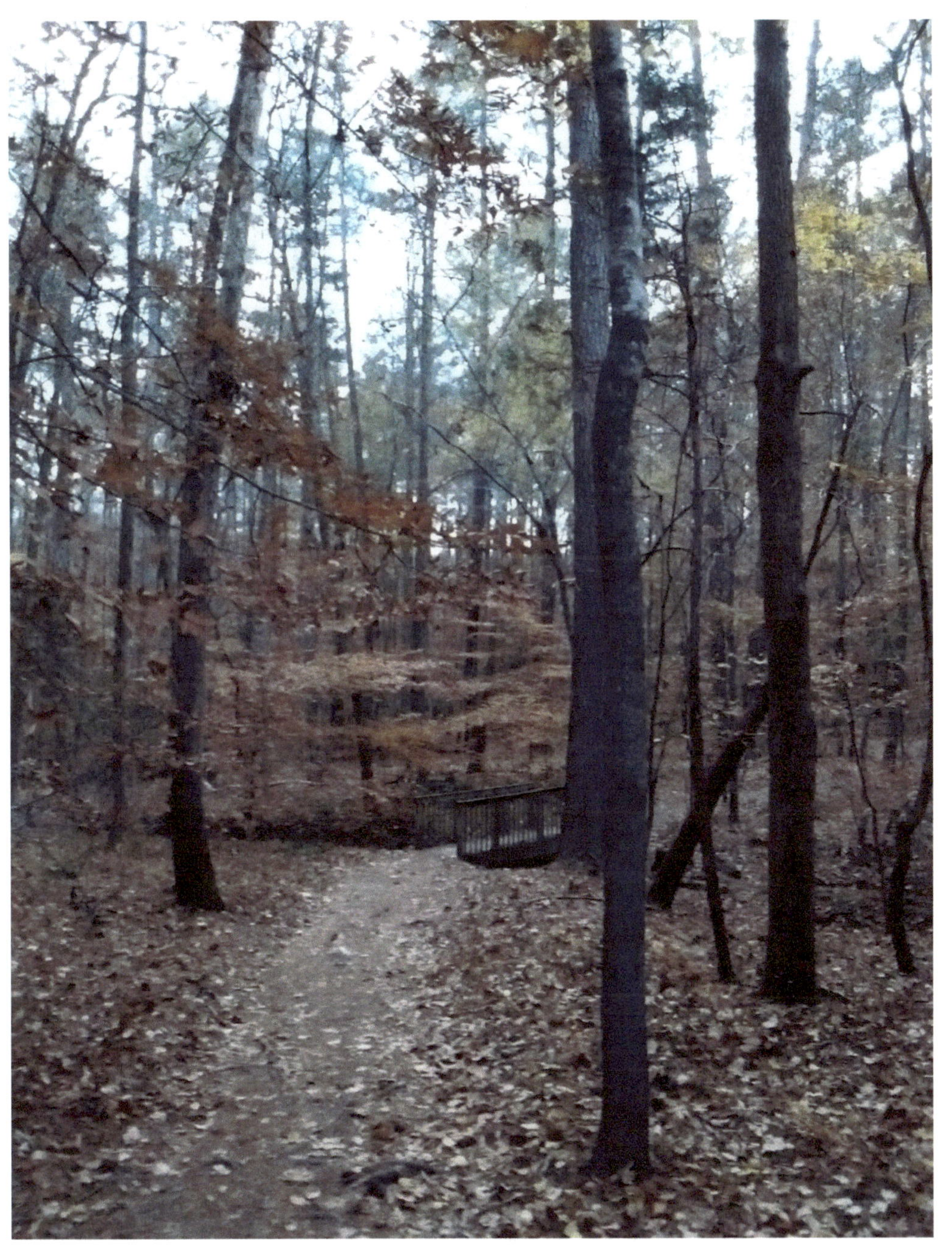

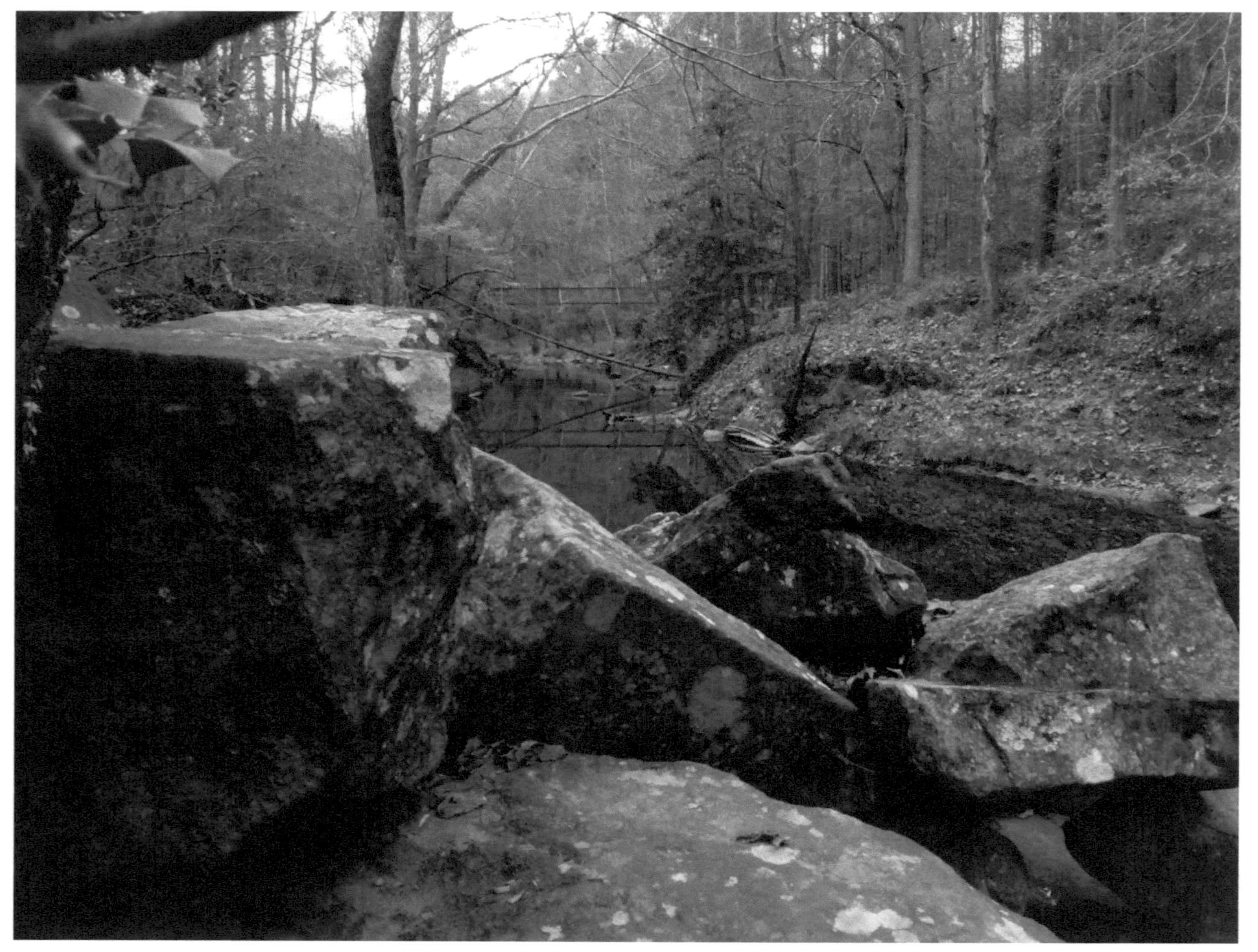

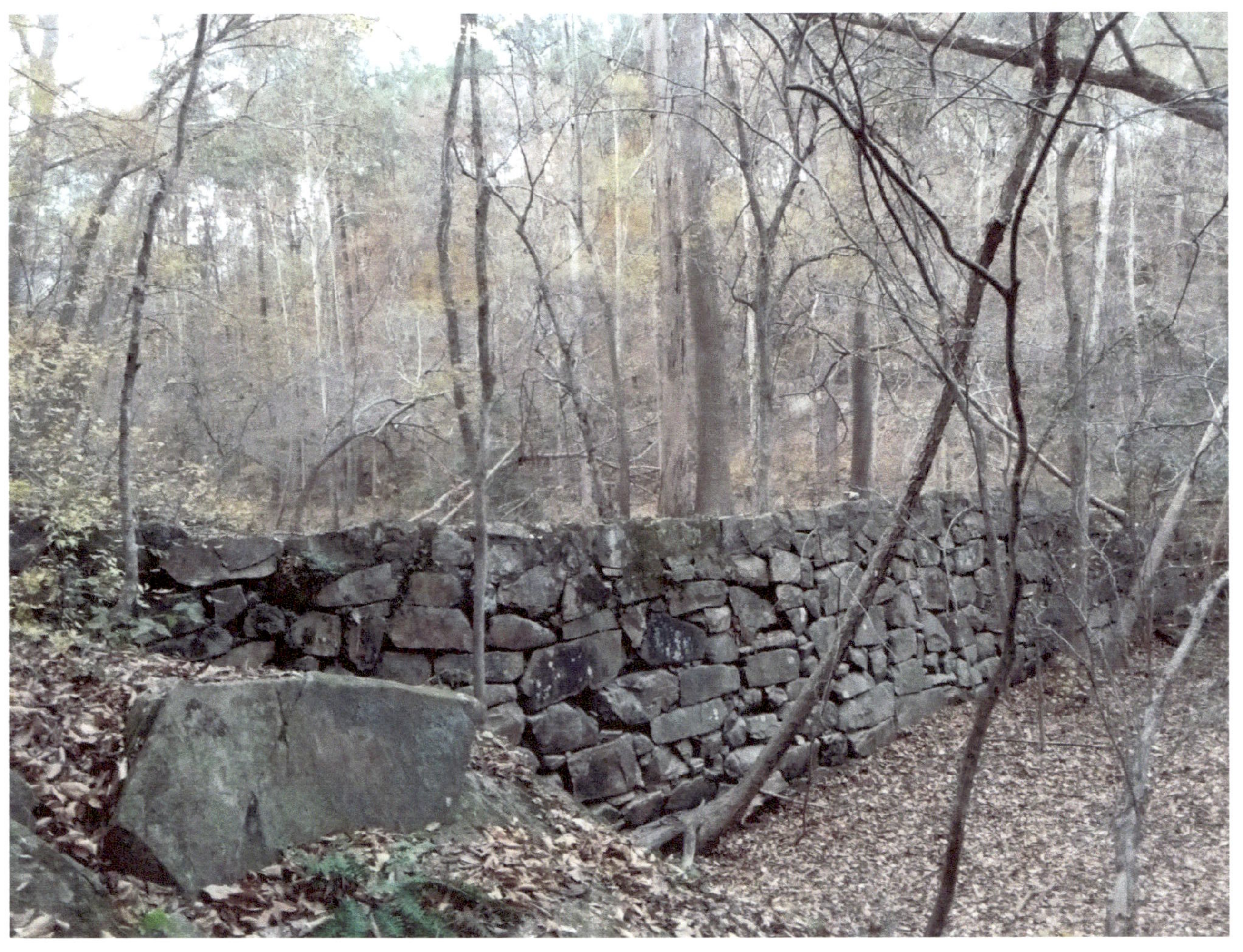

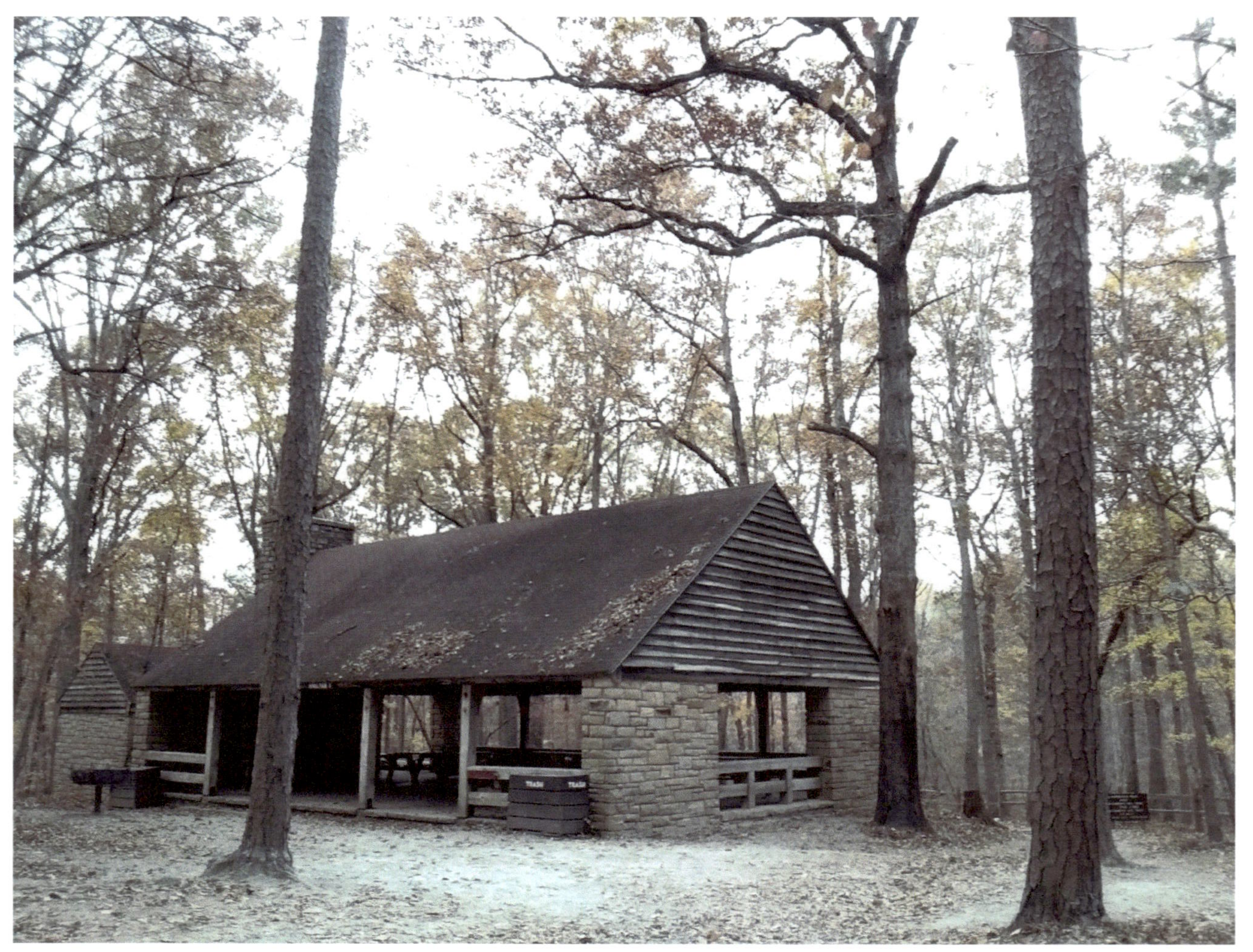

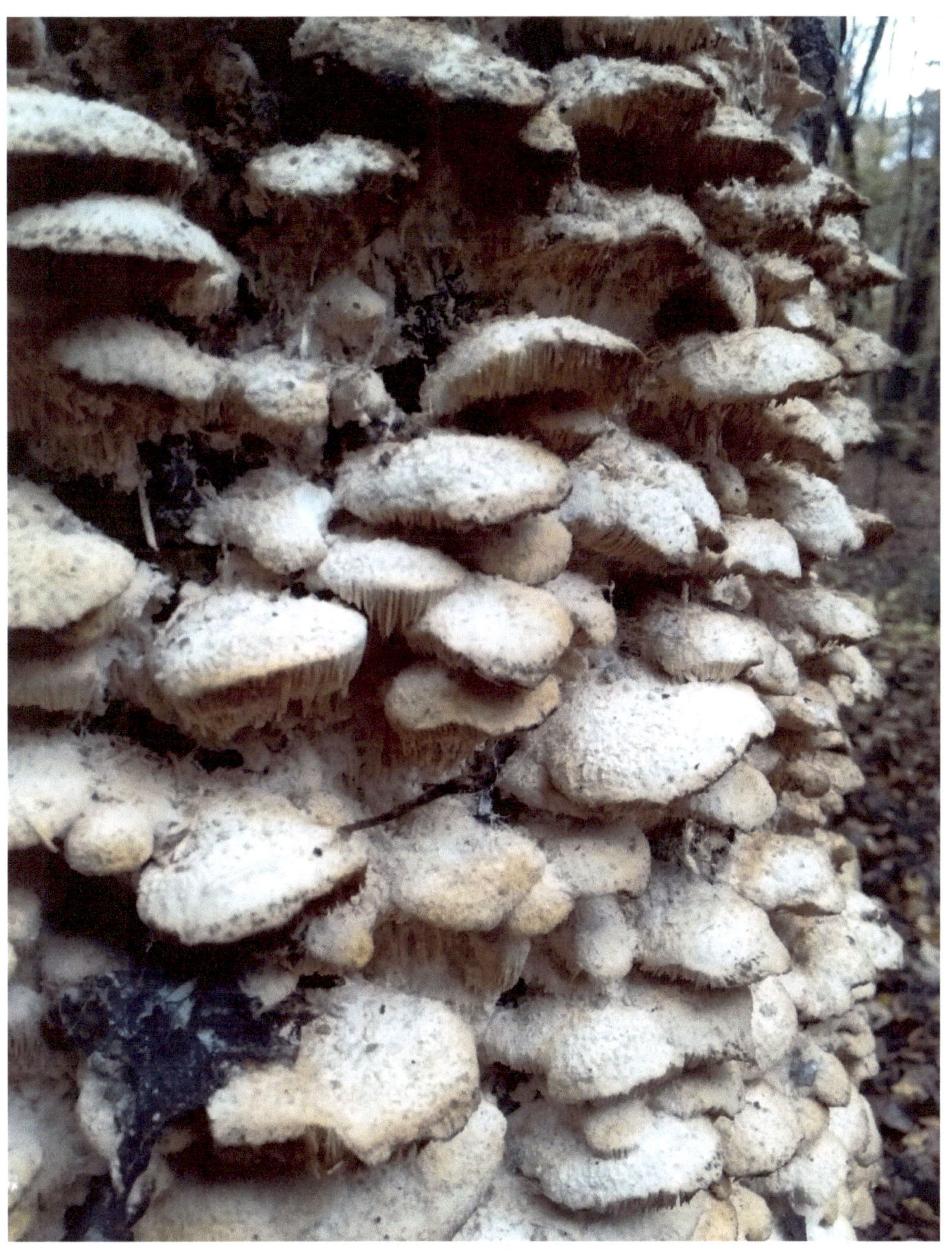

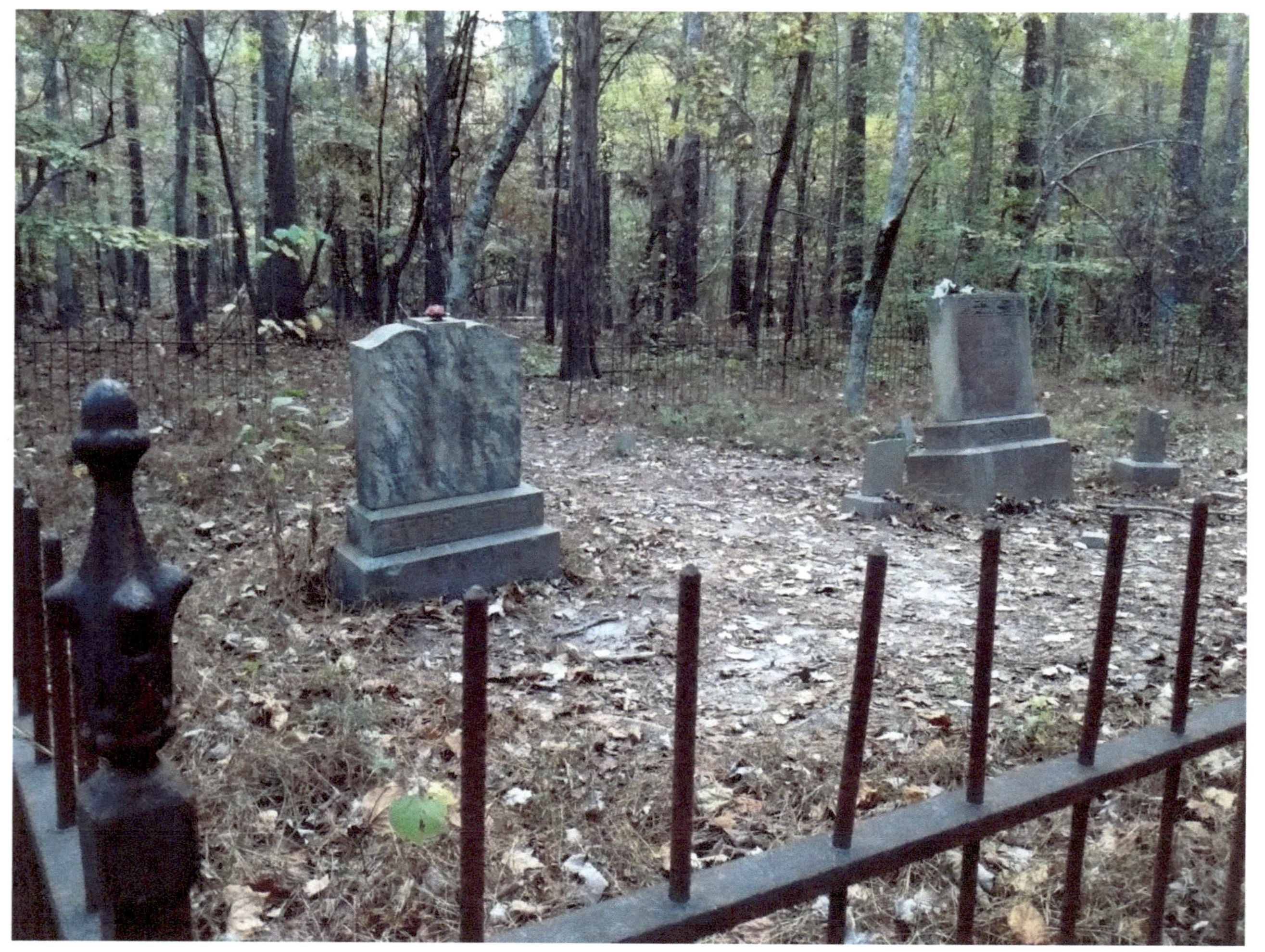

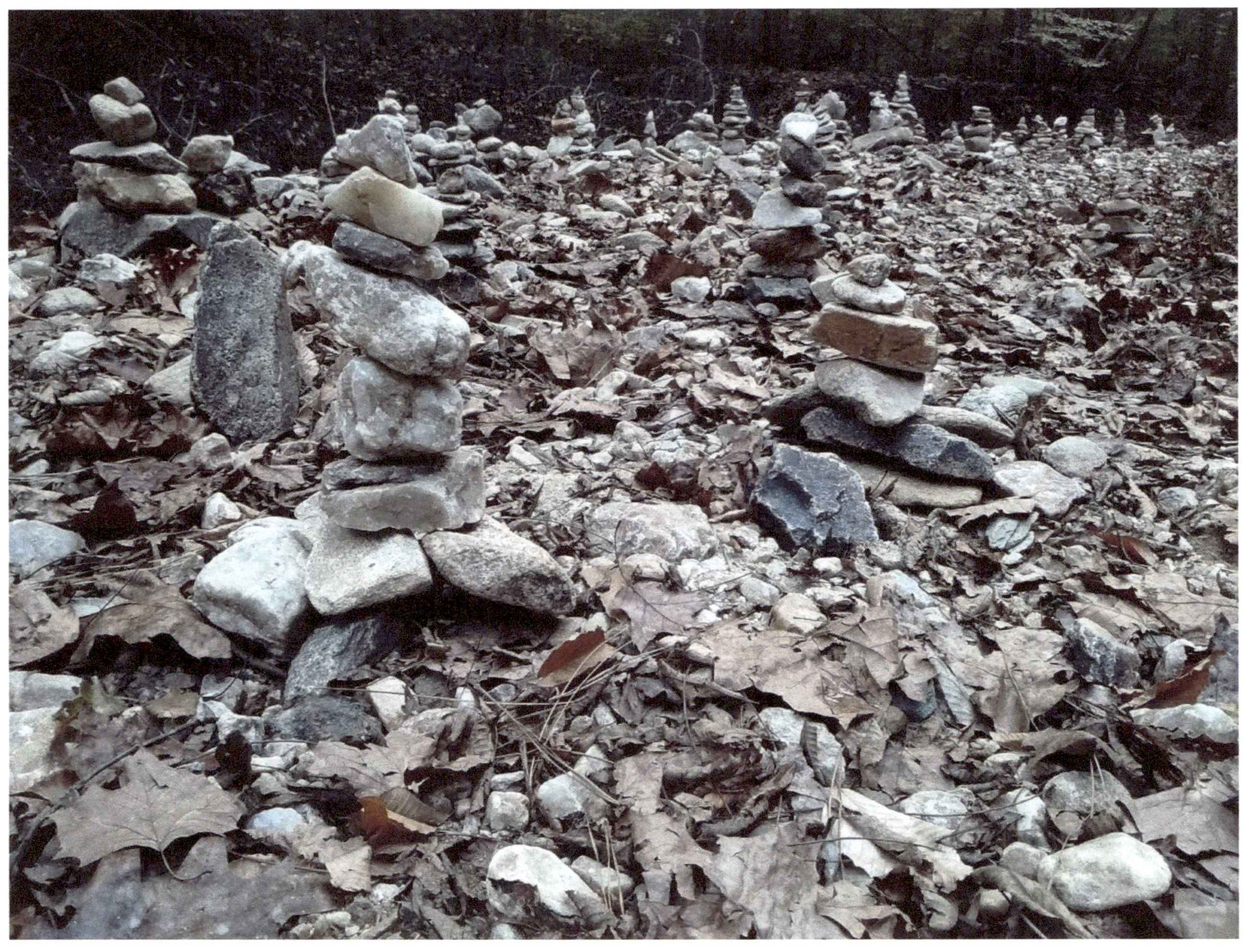

Check out my other books available.

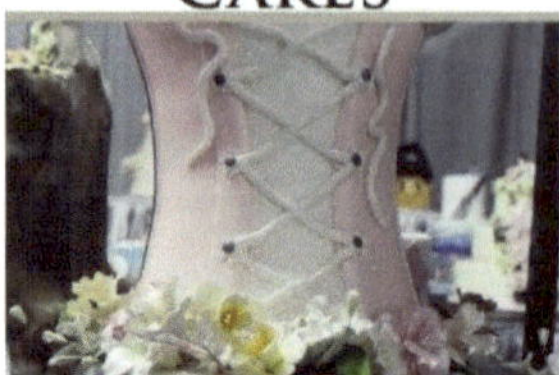

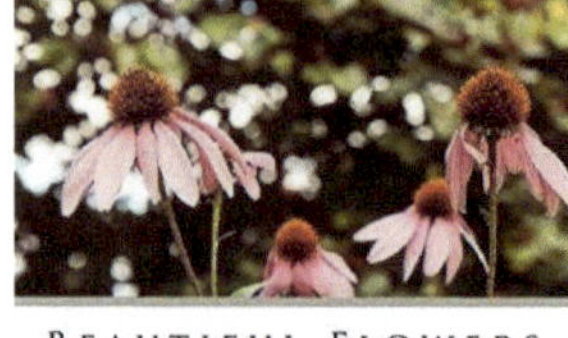

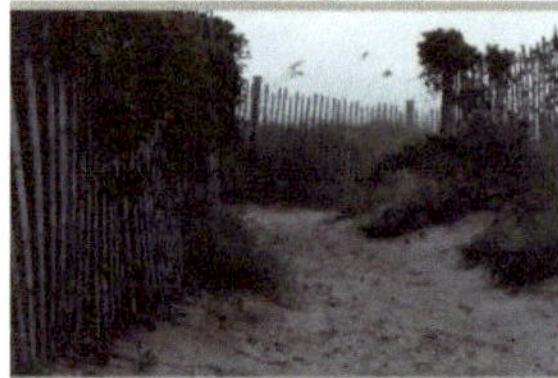

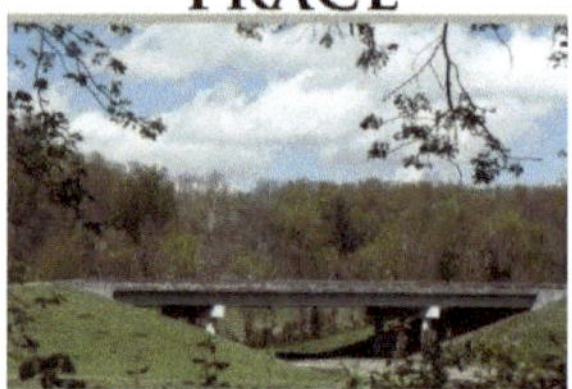

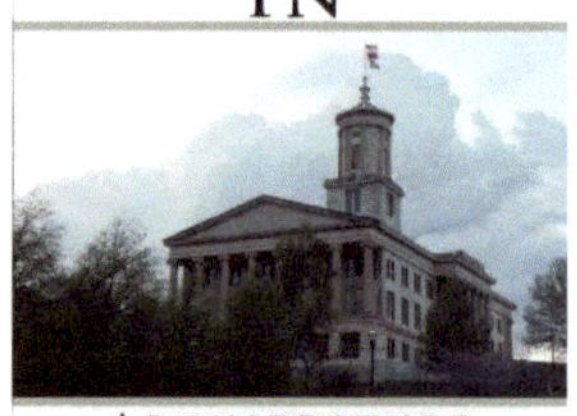

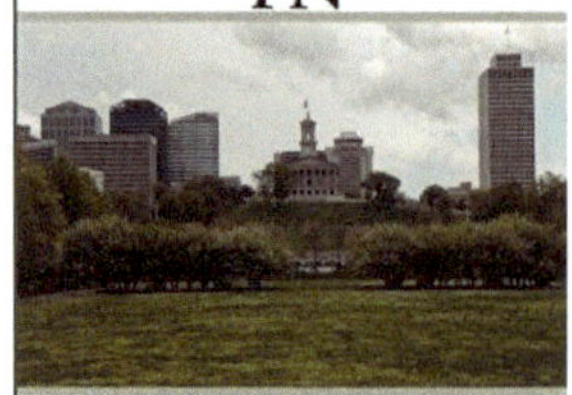

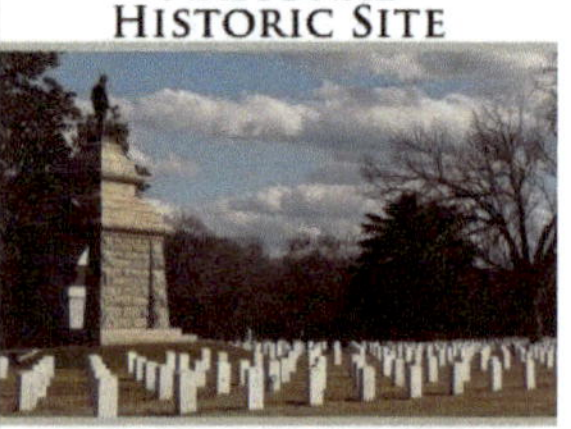

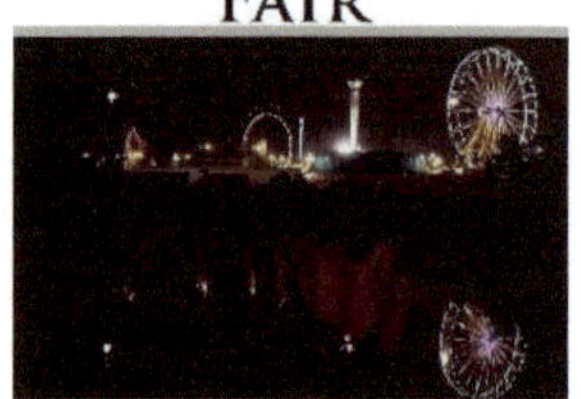

The end.